WITHDRAWN

THE IMPOSSIBLE VICTORY

The Impossible Victory

A personal account of the
Battle for the River Po

BRIAN HARPUR

HIPPOCRENE
BOOKS, INC.

First published in the United States 1981 by

HIPPOCRENE BOOKS INC.
171 Madison Avenue
New York, N.Y. 10016

PRINTED IN THE UNITED STATES OF AMERICA
9 8 7 6 5 4 3 2 1

I dedicate this book to the men of Princess Louise's Kensington Regiment with whom I had the privilege of serving in World War II.

I would also like to take this opportunity of thanking the great many friends, colleagues and kind people who helped in its compilation by offering me both verbal and written anecdotal and historical material and, in particular, Mrs Marie Overland who spent innumerable hours deciphering my almost illegible manuscript in her spare time and correcting and typing it for me.

BVCH
November 1979

Message from Prime Minister, Winston Churchill,
to Field-Marshal Alexander dated 29th April 1945

'I rejoice in the magnificently planned and executed operations of the Fifteenth Group of Armies, which are resulting in the complete destruction or capture of all the enemy forces south of the Alps. That you and General Mark Clark should have been able to accomplish these tremendous and decisive results against a superior number of enemy divisions, after you have made great sacrifices of whole armies for the Western Front, is indeed another proof of your genius for war and of the intimate brotherhood in arms between the British Commonwealth and Imperial forces and those of the United States. Never, I suppose, have so many nations advanced and manoeuvred in one line victoriously . . .'

Contents

List of Illustrations

A map of the campaign area appears on page 147

Introduction

This is basically the story of a strange and heroic battle which brought to a triumphant end the bitter Italian campaign in World War II. Nobody knows much about it. It appears to have had no lengthy accolade from a gifted pen. It has been skimped by historians.

It does not even have a name because the battleground where its climax was intended to be enacted became instead the venue for a colossal anti-climax.

I choose to call it the Battle for the River Po.

For reasons which will become clear later it was not just a battle in the conventional sense of blood and bullets. It was one, the sombre prospect of which sent a shudder of fear through a million soldiers on both sides taking part in a way no other battle had ever done.

It was a battle in which all the arts and principles of warfare were deployed damn near to perfection. It demonstrated a degree of co-operation between the troops of many nations and the skills of their commanders to a degree which will surely not be seen again.

As an ordinary soldier pitchforked from civilian life into the bewildering activities of the army and peering through the fog of war with cracked binoculars I found myself obsessed with this particular battle. Even now more than thirty years later I still ponder upon its unique and bizarre aspects with awe and astonishment.

Technically, if the arithmetic of successful battle in terms of the numbers of men and machines required has any validity it should have been a dismal failure.

Politically, it should never have taken place at all. The Top Brass back in the corridors of power in Whitehall and Washington had determined that any undue activity in Italy at this stage of the war was to be deplored.

For all sorts of other reasons it seemed an impossible venture, not the least being that just before it was due to begin one of the corps commanders on the Allied side announced that he was going to pull out of it together with 100,000 men no less. The kind of news assuredly which must have sent a few high-ranking staff officers hurrying off to the latrine.

Indeed in the preceding months the Allied effort had been struck with other hammer blows when the equivalent of several small armies had been withdrawn from the Italian front to make what turned out to be arguably a quite unnecessary invasion of France.

I kept on asking myself 'how could the Allied armies in Italy, beleaguered as they were in appalling terrain, denuded, despairing, out-numbered, stale, "bomb-happy", and utterly war-weary win what surely must have been the war's most extraordinary battle?'

'How could they have hoped to defeat German armies skilfully led by generals of the quality of Kesselring and possessing not only very brave resourceful and experienced troops but also occupying extremely well prepared defensive positions in depth along the entire front?'

Yet the fact is they did. On 9th April 1945 four generals, Alexander, Mark Clark, McCreery and Truscott, staged an astonishing coup which brought about in less than a fortnight the first major surrender of the German armies in World War II. A million laid down their arms.

'A text book battle,' said Field Marshal Alexander.
'A great feat of arms,' said General Sir Richard McCreery.
'One of the finest battles ever fought,' said General Mark Clark.

As usual, Winston Churchill had the last word when he wrote to Alexander '. . . This great final battle in Italy will long stand out in history as one of the most famous episodes in the Second World War.'

I was determined to learn as much as I could about this 'great final battle' and so as the years passed by I have had long personal correspondence and conversations with Alexander, Mark Clark, McCreery and many others. What they told me and the manner of their telling have been very revealing, not only in relation to the narrow consideration of the Battle for the River Po itself, but also in relation to their characters and attitudes and to their previous stinging controversies, contretemps and triumphs for which they were held responsible.

I never really knew what Alexander thought about Mark Clark's much publicised decision to go for Rome instead of cutting off the German retreat in June 1944, as Mark Clark had been expected to, until accidentally I had a conversation with him in a place called Benevento near Caserta in Italy.

I never really appreciated the extent of the contempt Mark Clark appeared to have had for Eisenhower until he took me into his private study in his home in the Citadel, Charleston, South Carolina, and showed me a selection of letters about the mishandling of the Anzio operation.

The one factor which, had it been discovered in time, could have enabled Montgomery to destroy Rommel's tanks entirely and to conclude the Battle of El Alamein a day earlier was revealed to me by General Sir Richard McCreery as we sat reminiscing together in the comfortable recesses of the chairs in the Cavalry Club in London some ten years later.

However, while these unsuspected glimpses of great men and great events may possibly illumine the odd dark corner of history, my main purpose in the ensuing chapters is to try and write in simple language the story of the Battle for the River Po so that those who were too young to be there or not even born then can share some fraction of my enthusiasm and fascination.

This will therefore be a highly personalised account, not only because I was there, but because I want to explain what that kind of war was all about, and why so many small and unrelated things like shaving in cold water, harnessing a reluctant mule, getting a letter from home, lying in a slit trench with a decomposed body, oiling a rifle, puffing furiously on a soggy cigarette, doing guard duty, starving to death, listening for the 'whoosh' of a shell, trying to stay awake at dawn, and always being got ready to do something two hours before it was necessary, conditioned the minds of the men who made victories possible.

So if there are any old sweats who find it boring to have things spelt out please bear with me so that those who never went through our school of experience can get some insight into the way platoons and armies marched and what we mean when we talk of DUKWs, Fantails, Flails, LST's, Mortars, Nebelwerfers to say nothing of Sparrow Fart.

1.   'The Goddam Troops'

'You can't fight a Goddam battle unless
you have the Goddam troops.'

US COLONEL NORTHERN APENNINES, 1944

A big six wheel truck went grinding up an icy track in the Apennines. Sitting behind the steering column was an enormous negro GI, tin helmet at a jaunty angle, a gold tooth showing where he bit on a fat cigar and a look of complete nonchalance on his face. Squatting at the side of the track was a dishevelled African soldier, his black face ashen with cold.

The truck stopped and the driver opened the window, flicked his cigar ash disdainfully and after surveying his coloured cousin for a few pregnant seconds he enquired patronisingly :

'Hello, savage – where's yo' spear ?'

He then got down from the truck and shared some hot coffee and biscuits with his less fortunate friend. No offence taken.

If there was one thing the Allies learnt in Italy it was co-operation.

Eventually the essential logic of co-existence depending on a measure of confidence and trust in each other's professionalism had seeped through. But it must be said that the prejudices and bigotry characteristic of so many individuals as well as of whole nations were never far from the background. The conceit of the Allied armies in Italy founded often on misconceptions about their respective superiorities had to be endured as well as be believed.

The British fortified by the success of the Eighth Army from El Alamein onwards had considerable contempt for the 'Yanks' as soldiers. They would recall with patronising pomposity how time and time again the Guards had to be sent into battle in Tunisia in 1943 to

15

recapture the ground the scruffy and undisciplined GI's had not had the guts to hold. The fact that this was the arena in which the first largely untrained and raw American divisions to make an overseas invasion were committed against the seasoned veterans of Rommel's armies was overlooked, as was the fact that the British in their first baptism of fire did not do all that extraordinarily well in the debacle that led to Dunkirk.

The Americans displayed a certain arrogance about their superiority over the 'Limeys' who they thought were always dragging their feet and simply were not to be trusted. The Americans, they liked to think of themselves, thought big, fought big, and got results fast. Their 'get up and go' philosophy was in sharp contrast with the 'pussy-footing – tap on the window with a wet sponge' approach of the lousy 'Limeys'. In fact some of the most spectacular coups of the war were conceived and carried out by the British, as for example in their surge through the Liri Valley and thrust for the Argenta Gap which will be described later. It was an American general with mostly ill-directed American formations who botched the Anzio operation with such dire results. The truth of course is that both sides had their glories and disasters in a manner contradicting their so-called national characteristics.

I remember a nasty engagement on the Northern Apennines in the autumn of 1944 when I was despatched to offer machine-gun support for an American battalion attempting to capture a gigantic mountain called 'point 508'. In my eagerness to secure maximum information and carry out a detailed reconnaissance I dashed a long way ahead with my driver in my jeep. Eventually I caught up with the American colonel in a farmhouse and introduced myself. He was a stocky balding little man of middle age with bulging eyes and covered in mud and sweat. His helmet swayed drunkenly on his head as he pored over his maps in the softening twilight filtering on to the table. He let me wait for a few minutes as he muttered curses and imprecations to a few tired and dejected officers around him.

'We gotta take that knob,' he kept on repeating. 'Where's Joe?' he kept on asking.

Suddenly he whipped round on me and bellowed, 'How many men ya got?' I said I had two platoons. His eyes glistened. 'We can do with them right now, Barker,' (he had misheard my name) 'and get them in there' – he jabbed an unlit cigar in the general area of some high ground nearby – 'in fifteen minutes.' There was an embarrassing silence.

'What ya waiting for?' he demanded.

I explained a little diffidently that I had come in advance and my chaps, jolly decent chaps they were too I was tempted to say, could not be with me for at least two hours. 'Goddammit,' he shouted, 'you can't fight a Goddam battle unless you have the Goddam troops.'

Before the irrefutable logic of this observation could sink in somebody at the door interrupted with 'Here comes Joe' and the colonel rushed outside.

I followed him and witnessed a remarkable scene which contrasted forever in my memory the way Americans and the British do things.

The British Army has been doing things by numbers for centuries. There is a prescribed drill for literally everything you do from the manoeuvring of armies to the fixing of the humble bayonet. Let me hasten to add that the British Army has got it right. Only in this way can the best possible reflex to all situations be predicted but also in terms of communication it provides a certain clarity and unambiguity which enable even generals to comprehend what they think they should be doing.

In this respect there was no function which had a more precise and undeviating formula than the issuing of battle orders. One was drilled over and over again to deliver these either verbally or in writing under five headings.

INFORMATION (first about dispositions and numbers of one's own troops and then of the enemy).

INTENTION (explain nature of objective to be taken and its location and always use the word 'will' e.g. 'X Platoon *will* attack' not hopes to' nor 'intends to subject to the enemy beating the living daylights out of us first' or any nonsense like that).

METHOD (describe the plan in such reasonable detail that subordinate commanders could pass it on without any misunderstanding).

ADMINISTRATION (here the arrangements for food, petrol, oil, ammunition, and for any special equipment are outlined).

INTERCOMMUNICATION (the location of the various headquarters, boundaries, signal frequencies are noted).

This barrage of controlled verbiage then had to be concluded with two mandatory rituals. One was to ask 'Any questions'? and the other was the command 'Synchronise watches'. Both were wise precautions for obvious reasons.

Therefore, I waited for the colonel to issue orders to Joe in time-honoured fashion. Metaphorically, I sat back in the cosy security of my subconscious anticipation of Information – Intention – Method – Administration – Inter-Communciation – Any Questions and Synchronise Watches. There was no other way it could or should be done. I was wrong.

'For Chrissake, Joe, what kept ya?' the colonel bellowed down the hill. Joe, a young, boyish, slim and somewhat dejected figure, stopped in his tracks. He had a hard black stubble of two days' unshaven hair around his chin which emphasised the pallor and fatigue of his eyes and face. There was a slight pause while he transferred slowly what might have been a map case from one hand to the other. Before the dialogue got any further there was a roar like an express train overhead followed by another and yet another. The Germans were pitching into us with some of their biggest shells. At the same time the staccato deep-throated 'crrump' of mortar bombs was heard all round us. To a man we flung ourselves to the ground. It all stopped as suddenly as it began.

The colonel was first on his feet. He did not waste any time enquiring about our wellbeing or anything as superfluous as that. He peered the fifty yards down the hill where an uncertain Joe was raising himself wearily on to his legs.

'Listen, Joe, I've gotta special assignment for you,' shouted the colonel in a stentorian delivery which must have kept any enemy within half a mile au fait with the impending plan. The colonel paused for a dramatic split second between the words 'special' and 'assignment' in a way which suggested that Joe was the luckiest guy in the world to be given it.

As if conscious of his dictum that one cannot fight a Goddam battle unless one has the Goddam troops, he added, 'How many men ya got, Joe?'

Joe thought for a second: 'Ah reckon about seventeen, Colonel.'

The colonel nodded and then made his first and only concession to what might be called joint consultation.

'Do you reckon you can take that knob, Joe?'

He pointed to the massive rock tipped mountain which soared hundreds of feet immediately above us. As if to guide Joe in giving the appropriate answer he immediately added, 'We've gotta have that knob, Joe.'

Joe bent his head in tired affirmative. 'Ah reckon so, Colonel, ah reckon so.'

'Can you go in at 1930 hours?' asked the colonel. Then as an inducement he explained, 'I'll fix artillery support by then and give you as easy a ride as I can.'

There was a long pause. God knows what was going through Joe's mind as he assessed the chances of his seventeen men capturing a 'knob' which dominated this mountainous area. It was doubtful if five hundred men could do it. Indeed five hundred had already tried and failed.

Joe raised his head. I still see him as a pathetic but proud silhouette of the eternal soldier as he turned on his heels. 'OK, Colonel' was all he said. I had never heard orders before which so flouted the conventions and yet went so quickly to the heart of the matter. I felt very humble in the face of such heroism.

Events conspired to prevent my ever finding out how Joe fared. All I know is that at dawn the following morning I crawled under heavy shell-fire over the same ground with men of a British brigade who had been sent in to relieve the Americans, who had in fact succeeded in taking that hateful 'knob'. Everywhere the dead bodies of men like Joe and the Colonel lay like grotesque stepping stones on the way to their objective. Looking back I wonder if the Americans would have achieved their goal with far less casualties if they had waited for reinforcements and the formulation of a proper set-piece attack as the British would probably have done. Such a pause on the other hand could have enabled the enemy to re-group and consolidate the defence of the 'knob' when the carnage might have been even greater. It is impossible to say but my instinct tells me that in this instance the Americans were right. The longest way round is not always the shortest way home.

The prototype for each and every army has always been endowed with the somewhat affectionate anonymity of its most numerous component – the private soldier. In the forces of the United Kingdom he takes the pseudonym of a certain 'Thomas Atkins'. Thus the British 'Tommy'* is the cynosure for all people of the cheerful, self-effacing and indomitable human being that he has represented in two world wars.

The French equivalent is the *'poilu'* and the American is the immortal 'GI' derived from the initials of 'general issue' or 'Government Issue' with their conscious irony of being essential but very expendable.

To understand the real significance of the Battle for the River Po one has to grasp clearly not only the simple truth that one cannot fight

*TOMMY ATKINS – From Brewer's Dictionary of Phrase and Fable.
'Tommy or Tommy Atkins – A British private soldier, as a JACK TAR is a British sailor. At one time all recruits were served out with manuals in which were to be entered the name, age, date of enlistment, length of service, wounds, medals, and so on of the holder. With each book was sent a specimen form showing how the one in the manual should be filled in, and the hypothetical name selected was 'Thomas Atkins'.

a 'goddam' battle without the 'goddam' troops but also the multitude of little things which enable those 'goddam' troops of a score or more of different nationalities to work together and survive. Each and every one with the stubborn instinct of individuals was in essence a psychological problem, a supply problem, a logistical problem, a motivation problem, a religious problem, and when he was none of these he was dead. Even then he posed one last problem. His body had to be identified and sent back for burial and his personal effects had to be salvaged and listed. The final gesture was to despatch those which were appropriate to his next of kin with a letter of comfort from his commanding officer.

The Americans tackled the problem of their dead with such pragmatic efficiency that long after the armies had moved forward one could often find a solitary but determined GI moving forlornly around the mountains well to the rear dragging a reluctant mule behind him. His role was to locate the bodies of any stray GI's whether in makeshift graves or not, to disinter them, and bring them back to a central collection point.

So it will be appreciated that if the conflicting factors which any ordinary individual is heir to are multiplied a hundredfold or millionfold depending on the size of the formation or army taking the field, there has to be a basic organisation which can cope. The Greeks and the Romans, for example, quickly found out that if you start out with a small unit of say ten men and put them under the command of one man who in turn is responsible to a man in a slightly higher position who controls not one but three such units, then one can develop a chain of command whereby a hundred men can be fed, watered, trained and disciplined as an efficient fighting unit.

This concept has remained unchanged throughout the centuries and even to-day despite the advent of new requirements and technologies the chain of command closely resembles that of World War II and two thousand years before that of the Roman Legion. It is built roughly on the ten times table. All you have to remember is that the unit of ten men just referred to is called a section. Two or more sections are called a platoon. Two or more platoons (usually three) make a company and three or more companies (usually five and six) make a battalion. At this point because the number of troops have grown considerably some more are added to handle the discipline and administrative problems like the Regimental Police and Orderly Room Staff, so the strength of a battalion could be roughly 700 men – the equivalent of seventy of the original unit of measurement, the ten-man section.

Now it is just a short step in the progression to a whole army group. Two or more battalions (usually a minimum of three) make up a brigade. Two or more brigades provide a division, two or more divisions a corps, two or more corps an army, and finally two or more armies an army group.

But the catalogue of command does not rest there because at the higher echelons there are many specialist troops assigned to help the infantry in all their tasks, most of which involve close combat with the enemy. Make no mistake about it, the infantryman had the worst job as well as the most important job in the whole of the war. At the end of the day, often a long, frustrating, and very frightening day when he saw his comrades shot to pieces around him, and he knew it was his turn next, no ground was gained, no skirmish nor battle won, without that heroic and anonymous figure the ordinary infantryman winkling out his adversary at the point of his bayonet.

To give him close support in this crucial role a variety of skills were provided, usually at division level comprising for example a support group with medium machine guns, and heavy mortars, together with units of the Royal Artillery employing batteries of '25 pounder' and heavier guns, and all usually put at the disposal of brigades in convenient shapes and sizes according to battle requirements.

In addition there were other corps and divisional troops who were assigned to divisions and brigades who played equally important and courageous roles in Italy. Heavy tanks, light tanks and armoured cars were in constant demand. Many of these unlikely and unromantic vehicles which, although described as 'practically useless for stud purposes' by one disgruntled officer with an equestrian bias, manoeuvred in the name of the great cavalry regiments with all their fine traditions.

The Royal Engineers whose origins lay in their ability centuries ago to dig a sap or covered trench with a view to blowing up enemy fortifications from underneath were never more overworked. In some ways the 'sappers' made a more important contribution in support of the infantry than even the 'gunners' or any other arm of the Services. They did everything from mine lifting and bomb disposal to road maintenance. Their bridge building exploits, often in the teeth of fierce enemy action, alone made it possible for an advance to be made, and for vital supplies to be sustained.

The latter which ranged from socks to sandbags, from bullets to bombs, from provisions to petrol, were ferried forward to dumps within a mile or two of the front line by a great breed of drivers from the

Royal Army Service Corps, whose attachment to their duty and to the unit they served was a wonder to behold.

As you can imagine with so many troops being deployed in so many difficult ways and in so many different situations the one essential thing if you were to find out if you were winning or losing was to have an instant and widespread system of communication. Since wars first began this has always been a major pre-occupation with commanders at every level. It has taken many forms. Fast runners specially trained to carry long verbal messages, scouts riding horseback with their despatches, the heliograph, semaphore, the telegraph wire, and morse code all demonstrate at some stage that the necessity to communicate in war was the mother of their invention.

So evolved the Royal Corps of Signals and in every headquarters from battalion upwards a Signals Officer was on the establishment. He and his men made sure that from the outpost in the front line to the Army Group Headquarters, not only way back but sometimes in a different country, a line of communications by wireless and telephone was maintained. Every platoon had a wireless set with an operator, sometimes even sections, and in addition every unit from section upwards had a field telephone system installed within the hour by dedicated signallers who often spent a hazardous time not only out in the open laying their lines but in checking and repairing them following enemy shell and mortar fire.

But that is not the end of the story. All these men have got to be fed, to be given medical and dental attention, to be paid, and even entertained so you have the Army Catering Corps, the Royal Army Medical Corps, The Royal Army Pay Corps, and ENSA. Their guns, tanks, vehicles, ammunition, and thousands of bits of complicated equipment have to be checked, serviced and replaced so giving rise to the invaluable contribution made by the Royal Army Ordnance Corps, and highly trained electrical and mechanical engineers (REME) who thought nothing of going out into no-man's-land and hauling back broken-down tanks with winch and hoist from a strange monster called appropriately a 'tank recovery vehicle' whilst all the time under fire.

There are many more service units not mentioned here but by now you will understand that commanding any formation in battle could be a very daunting task. To say that the army was labour intensive is an understatement. For every infantryman climbing a mountain or crossing a river in anger, for every infantryman reaching his objective with a gory bayonet or a red-hot gun barrel on his shoulder, there were perhaps as many as twenty not only trying to ensure that he got there but eternally grateful that they were not infantrymen themselves.

So that you can better envisage the more human aspects of some of the events which are yet to be unfolded I can do no better than give you my own story of how I got involved. It is typical of the hundreds of thousands of Britons who were called to the colours from 'Civvy Street' and who in some miraculous fashion eventually became sufficiently proficient in the arts of war to be able to take their place with pride in such a classic battle as that for the River Po.

The training, trials, and tribulations I endured were no different from those shared by a million others. The strange things which happened to me as I struggled to find myself in the bewildering world of army life, and my thoughts and reactions as I encountered new problems and situations daily were much the same as befell any Tommy Atkins. Trivial as they may seem, they all conspired to equip one both mentally and physically over the years for that final battle.

2. 'What's for Duff?'

You have heard of people leading a sheltered life but mine was ridiculous. I was born in Dublin, Ireland's lovely Georgian city, on 16th April 1918. Both my parents were Irish and were typical products of the Victorian and Edwardian eras. My father was a Protestant clergyman who nursed his flocks in three little parishes in what was then called Queen's County and is now called Leix. Among my earliest memories of him are his attempts to teach me cricket in a cow field when he laboriously pulled a big roller over the unyielding turf to try and make a pitch. He then pushed a piece of wood into my hands which purported to be a bat and solemnly bowled slow erratic long hops with an old tennis ball which I invariably missed.

Again as a little toddler I remember him wheeling his heavy old bicycle up the drive to the Rectory as he returned from one of his innumerable visits to his three little churches and his parishioners scattered over thirty square miles in some of the loveliest but physically most demanding country in the whole of Ireland. He had a wonderful silver-coloured lamp in front lit by carbide and it was one of my joys to see him clean it out and catch the distinctive whiff of the vapour as he replenished it.

I recall coming down to breakfast on cold mornings and being greeted by the crackle and flame of a freshly lit fire in the dining room which sent glowing shadows dancing on the ceiling and reflected in turn on the willow-patterned plates. I was the youngest of the six children in the family gathered there and it was my job to warm a cushion at the fire for my mother to sit on. I used to hold it near the flames until it nearly singed while watching her lower herself slowly into her seat. I would then rush over to the back of her chair and insert the cushion under her posterior in the nick of time. A task of rare excitement and

24

job satisfaction. Father would then read a few words from the Bible followed by prayers when we knelt on the floor with our backs to the table and our heads and arms resting on our chairs.

My mother was a beauty in her day, at least so she assured us, and indeed the visible evidence even in her more advanced years confirmed that fact. She had quick wit, a rare sense of humour, and like so many mothers with large families she was long suffering and wise. She had a passion for bridge and for doing advanced crossword puzzles which she maintained literally to her dying day.

My first taste of martial life was provided by my eldest brother, Ernest, when I was five years old. Although only sixteen he lied about his age in order to volunteer for the First World War and had seen active service with the Royal Artillery in France. After the Armistice he graduated into railway construction in India and he came home on leave in 1923. He presented me with a little toy rifle, the barrel of which was made of shiny tin. 'Go and clean it,' he commanded, 'and then I will inspect it.' This I did conscientiously in the very unmilitary precincts of my mother's bedroom using the bottom of her soft flannelette nightdress for the purpose. I then paraded in the gravel drive outside the front of the Rectory while brother Ernest taught me to slope arms and to slow march, a discipline I relieved by some unorthodox fancy footwork whenever he averted his head, which on reflection I am sure he did in order to conceal his laughter.

My other brother, Douglas, used to enliven my existence by wheeling me up a sloping path adjoining the Rectory in my pram and then letting it go to see how fast and how far it could run downhill unattended. I will never forget the look of astonishment and concern on his face when, on what turned out to be the last occasion he did this because of my mother's irate intervention, he saw the pram suddenly change direction at high speed having been deflected by a stone. It crashed into the wall and I was suspended bottom up in my harness. As a result, I cannot even to this day fasten my seat belt without mixed emotions.

Apart from one or two other contretemps as when a cow tossed me over a fence by raising me like a forklift truck by my jersey (an article of clothing which has taken an honoured place in the family history as 'the little grey gansey') which she gathered gently on the ends of her horns.

My three sisters, Vi, Edith and Grace, were all pretty, intelligent and attractive creatures whose presence at Church on Sundays must have done as much to ensure the attendance of male parishioners both young and old as the bravura of my mother's interpretation of Hymns Ancient and Modern coaxed from the gallant harmonium and my father's splendid but somewhat solemn sermons.

So you will gather from these not very remarkable incidents that we were a healthy, rumbustious, and happy family which did little to prepare me for Life except to endow me perhaps with a flexible outlook and a naive trust in people in general which was not a bad thing.

In 1925 we moved from our beloved Rectory to Dublin as my father, worn out by the cares of his office and his over-conscientious discharge of his duties, was forced to retire. He died of a stroke two years later but not before bequeathing me the best piece of business advice I ever heard. He used to call me 'my little man' and one day he felt he had to intervene when I was having a furious row with another eight-year-old about the division of some toy soldiers. After satisfactory arbitration he put his hands on my shoulders and looked down on me from his six foot height. His eyes ennobled by lines of suffering and topped by thick white well groomed eyebrows bored into mine.

'Ah my little man,' he said gently, 'whenever you do a deal make sure you leave enough for the other man,' and then he added with the hint of a twinkle, 'and make sure the other man leaves enough for you.'

At the age of thirteen I made my first real break from home. I was sent to a school in the North of Ireland called Portora Royal School, in Enniskillen, Co Fermanagh. This town is unique in having given its name to two great regiments, the Fusiliers and Dragoons. It also enjoys a unique setting in the beautiful undulating countryside which frames the wonderful waters of Lough Erne and its hundreds of enchanting islands.

My brother Douglas saw me off at the railway station in Dublin. He sensed my apprehension. 'You will find it a bit strange at first,' he conceded cheerfully, 'but don't be afraid to stand up for yourself. Above all when you play your first game of rugger play like hell.'

I can see him now waving to me as the train pulled out in a flurry of steam. He was then an undergraduate of Trinity College, Dublin, reading agriculture. He suddenly hit a religious phase following which he changed course and graduated in Divinity. During the war he carried out missionary work in Ceylon and finally died as the popular incumbent of a parish in St Albans, Hertfordshire, as a result of over-work and worry about his family and his flock as his father had done before him.

My first letter home to my mother from Portora which she kept was full of self-pity. The realisation that I was not the only pebble on the beach was echoed in a few words I had written and which my mother delighted in playing back to me years later. They were 'what am I among so many'. This was not a question but a somewhat pretentious admission by a homesick schoolboy that adolescence had begun.

It was not long either before I discovered that not only was I very small fry but I was also a coward. Far from standing up for myself I found myself joining the ranks of those who had the collective courage to taunt boys who were less able to stand up for themselves than I was. It was neither serious nor vicious but just the same I knew that morally I was wrong. Equally on the rugger field I dreaded the physical contact of tackling and while I could give a reasonable simulation of falling on the ball in the face of the flying feet of the opposing forwards I made sure it was sufficiently ineffective to avoid my being hurt. Having been brought up on the literature of G. A. Henty and of tales of 'derring-do' of World War I to say nothing of the fine moral code engendered by the stories of the youthful heroes in the *Magnet* and *Champion* and other schoolboy magazines, I had nothing but contempt for myself. Frankly, I was a downright funk and the fact that I overcame it to some small degree was mainly attributable to the paradox that I had not got the moral courage to opt out of certain situations in front of other people.

On the whole my school days were happy days, and there were two things not enjoyed by most which perhaps gave me a bit of an edge when it came to the ultimate test of battle. In my final term I was made Head Prefect when I acquired the first real inklings of responsibility and of man management. The school also boasted an OTC, the abbreviation for 'Officers Training Corps', in which I rose to the giddy heights of corporal. It taught me very little about the war as I was to know it, but it gave me the hell of a good introduction to the kind of discomfort which war is all about.

By the time the Second World War started I had reached a stage in my business career where but for its intervention I seemed destined to achieve inconspicuous mediocrity. A few years before I had joined Associated Newspapers Limited as a messenger boy and filing clerk on the London *Evening News* and had gradually worked my way up via every humble job going until I became a junior salesman selling spaces to advertisers in the *Daily Mail*. Not all that promising, but with £5 per week plus a bit of hard earned commission I was able to survive, and have enough left over to take a girl to the pictures and have a drink with the lads once a week.

No sooner had Prime Minister Chamberlain announced that we were at war with Germany than I walked out of the office to join up. It stands to the eternal credit of the great paternal organisation for which I worked that far from taking exception to my abrupt behaviour they kept me on half pay throughout the six long weary years which lay ahead and offered a better job to me immediately on my return.

My thought was to join the Royal Air Force because I had a vague recollection of a first cousin, the son of my father's only sister, who was then serving with such distinction that he ultimately attained the very highest honours, and I felt that flying must be in the family. The recruiting office was in Kingsway and I shall never forget my dismay when I was told by a poker-faced sergeant that there were no vacancies. There and then I concluded that if I was going to be 'grounded' it might as well be the Army for me. So in the autumn of 1939 I found myself trudging with my battered suitcase into the depot of the Middlesex Regiment at Mill Hill in North London, together with an intake which provided prime examples of race, class, creed, and villainy. Within a few days I had sustained a series of shocks which left me in no doubt about the Facts of Life and the sheltered existence I had led. It was then, did I but know it, that my grooming for the final battle in Italy started and for hundreds of thousands like me.

We were conducted to our barrack rooms, issued with mess tins (those rectangular metal containers which housed one's shaving kit and socks when not in use for tea and stew) and ordered to parade at the cookhouse. As we edged forward in line, a very tall, thin, morose-looking lad stood forlornly in front head and shoulders above the rest. A few paces behind him a cheerful little cockney who fixed him with an eager eye and said in ringing tones, 'Hey, Lofty, give us a bit of brown.' The assembled company burst out laughing. I was considerably disconcerted to find that I seemed to be the only one who did not know what it meant. Even now I am not all that sure but at the time I sensed it was very rude, and I was deeply shocked.

Within an hour the next blow fell when we were whipped in and out of the barber's shop and shorn of all our treasured hair to within half an inch of our scalps. It might have been just a little more tolerable if the mind dulling routine of a few days in the Army had taken place beforehand but to travel hopefully and arrive as an individual and then to be reduced by a savage haircut to a convict symbol or cypher all in the same day was cruel.

By the evening we had been issued with our uniform kit and equipment, we had had our 'drop your trousers and cough' medical, we had filled in forms including 'next of kin' and had been given our first rudimentary lessons in marching in step by the traditional belligerent bully of a sergeant-major. I was miserable, crestfallen, and shaken to the core.

There were thirty of us bedding down that night on straw palliasses and I imagined, probably with some conceit, that I was more of a fish out of water than any of them. Their attitudes, oaths, and ribald conversation were utterly foreign to me. Half the time I could understand neither their pronunciation nor their vocabulary. They did not seem to be heir to any of the civilised procedures such as folding clothes or cleaning teeth with which one associated the ritual of going to bed.

I felt isolated and very depressed. 'So this is the Army, God how awful,' I thought. Then in a very uncharacteristic fit of desperation and defiance I did two of the only brave things which were not forced on me I ever did in my life. I undressed and as unselfconsciously as possible I put on a pair of pyjamas. I then knelt by my bed, a habit I had long forgotten, and said my prayers. It was only when I had sidled quietly into bed and pulled the coarse blankets around me that I realised that neither of my actions had provoked any comment nor ridicule if indeed they had been noticed at all. I felt a little ashamed. Perhaps they were not such bad chaps after all. My education had begun.

In the days that followed we were instructed, drilled, and generally chased from dawn to dusk so that as a platoon of raw private soldiers we not only drew together against the common tyranny of 'fatigues' which included the soul-destroying task of peeling a ton of intractable potatoes in icy water and incessant guard duties, but we actually started to volunteer to help each other out. Comradeships and teamwork had set in.

Another curious phenomenon was how in small things a spirit of competition arose between individuals in the platoon. The irksome tasks of cleaning equipment, shining buttons, and bringing the toe caps of one's boots to glossy brilliance which was achieved by burning the leather and then rubbing in polish for hours on end, (a process for some strange reason called 'gimping') provided the pegs on which great rivalry hung.

As one of the most naive of private soldiers I fell for every trick in the Army's book. 'Am I hurting you,' the sergeant would bellow in my ear from behind. 'No, sergeant,' was the apprehensive reply. 'Well, I ought to be, because I'm standing on your bleeding hair.' This old Army chestnut retold countless times which was simply the Army's way of telling one that a tiny speck of hair had been spotted below one's cap, actually happened to me. It was new to me then, as indeed was the dialogue between me and the same sergeant which went something like this, as he pressed his face against mine in a menacing eyeball to eyeball confrontation.

'Wot's your name, lad?' he articulated in a high-pitched hiss.

'Harpur,' I said nervously.

There was a pause. 'Wot's that again?' he hissed.

'Harpur,' I offered even more nervously while raising my eyebrows with a little twitch of the head by way of mute apology.

There was a slightly longer pause while with his face still glued to mine he allowed his eyes to roll ominously down the line of the rest of the platoon who were standing with some considerable expectation of drama rigidly to attention. Nobody moved a muscle.

'Stand still all of yer,' he enjoined. Then he stepped back and ostentatiously inspected me from head to foot. A look of suppressed triumph swept his craggy features as suddenly he thought of something.

Tucking his cane under his arm he asked with sarcastic solicitude, 'Am I to understand that as you being an 'arper you might play the 'arp?'

Loath to disillusion him I shook my head a little sadly.

'Stand still,' he bellowed. 'Perhaps you like the 'arp?' he coaxed.

Not wishing to invite another bellow I never moved an eyelid. Suddenly he addressed the whole platoon. 'Orl right then. Pay attention, orl of yer. Do any of yer like music?'

The widening of the terms of reference caused me to reflect upon my amateurish attempts to imitate the rhythmical precision of Charlie Kunz on the piano and of my passion for Ambrose and his Band. My hand shot up almost involuntarily.

The sergeant pounced on me. 'Right then, Private 'Arper. Report to me after parade to move a piano into the NAAFI.' As I said, I fell for everything. It never occurred to me for one moment that a liking for music was the necessary qualification for lugging a piano around. Army humour had a blunt uncompromising quality which turned boys into grown men overnight.

Nowhere was it more happily cradled than in the mess hall where one had what passed for breakfast, dinner, and tea. The main meal, dinner, was the occasion for a visit by the Orderly Officer and Orderly Sergeant for the day who would thread their way between tables asking perfunctorily, 'Any complaints?' Once in reply to this question a trembling new recruit rose to his feet and pointing to a gelatinous blob in his mess tin said, 'Yessir, I can't eat this fish.'

The officer looked at him coldly. 'Can't eat fish eh, that's not a complaint, that's a MISFORTUNE.' The discomfited soldier sat down while the officer and his expressionless entourage swept on.

The remark which set the seal on the comical reflex of Tommy Atkins as he became the victim of unyielding routine came to me at dinner one day. While trying to remember the menu one could expect for that particular day, the only certainty being that scme sort of boiled pudding would make an appearance as the last course, I turned to my neighbour and surprised myself by asking what there was for dessert.

'You mean what's for duff,' he responded gloomily.

However, behind all the banter and bullshit the basic weapon training was given during an increasing number of hours each week. We were told that one's rifle was one's best friend and we were issued with a pull-through consisting of a long string with a weight at one end and a loop at the other. In the latter was inserted a strip of flannel measuring about 4″ by 2″ which with an accuracy not always associated with Army nomenclature was referred to as 'four by two'. One put a little oil on the flannel and dropping the weighted end down the barrel one pulled the cord through again and again until the barrel was shining bright. Oiling the breech, checking the magazine which held five bullets, and rubbing down the stock with an oily rag completed a programme which the soldier performed probably more often than any other throughout the whole of his service.

The mystery of the Vickers water-cooled medium machine gun was also explored. While most of the county regiments of England were infantry, there were four which provided machine-gun battalions, namely Devonshire, Cheshire, Northumberland, and my own regiment, the Middlesex.

It was a curious weapon in that it resembled closely the old Maxim which was a throw-back to the early days of this century and World War I. Its main fascination probably stemmed from the fact that it was liable at any time to suffer from at least one of twenty different stoppages which had to be diagnosed by a series of complicated procedures and the appropriate 'IA', as the immediate emergency action was called, then applied. The most common stoppage resulted from the belt holding the bullets being fed in crookedly causing a jam. The 'IA' which one was taught instantly to apply regardless was to ease back the crank handle which was situated on the right hand side of the rear casing. This withdrew the firing mechanism called the lock. At the same time one pulled the belt sideways with the left hand and gave the crank a sharp tap forward again with the right. It usually worked, and the machine gunner carried with him to eternity the three word drill 'ease-pull-tap' which was dinned into him incessantly from the very start of his apprenticeship.

Despite the lovable eccentricities the weapon was quite efficient. It was mounted on a heavy tripod weighing about 50 pounds and had a range of two miles or more. Not only could it be fired direct at targets but also by the use of instruments it could fire by night or from behind cover at targets which the gunner could not see. In this respect it performed a role as sophisticated as that of the Royal Artillery. The infantry had a light machine gun called a Bren which was much more portable and was fired in short bursts almost entirely for close-range work.

As the weeks passed one sensed that the imposition of predictable routine, the gathering of knowledge, the growing familiarity with marching, drilling, weaponry, and the way the Army did everything in general, had conspired to provide an essential ingredient for one's future survival. One's biggest battle was then with the boredom of doing endless fatigue duties, guard duties, and the eternal inspections of rifles, feet, hair, belts, straps, packs, beds, blankets, boots, pay books, barrack rooms, and you name it. Whether you were born with it or it was issued to you by the Army it had to be inspected severally and collectively fifty times a week.

The pièce de résistance was one's personal kit inspection which came round at least every ten days or so. One had to lay out very precisely each article of clothing and equipment on one's bed in a design calculated to give absolute uniformity all along the room. Any deviation from this promptly caused one to be put on a 'fizzer' or 'charge', resulting in some punishment like sweating round the parade ground at the double with full pack on one's shoulders or being confined to barracks for three days. The Army never allowed one to forget that care of personal equipment was a prime duty, not so much because the taxpayer paid for it but because a slovenly and badly kitted soldier was more likely to be a dead one.

Indeed the personal belongings of the soldiers which had to be numerous enough to give him a fighting chance of survival in any permutation of weather and battle, and yet had to be compressed into one shoulder pack and one small sausage-shaped hold-all need some explanation if one is to grasp the human significance of the rest of this narrative.

His hardware included his rifle, bayonet, steel helmet, clips of ammunition, knife, fork, spoon, mess tin, mug, spare metal buttons, needle (and thread). His 'soft' ware included three pairs of redoubtable socks, three khaki shirts (whenever an officer questioned a missing shirt on kit inspection the time-honoured reply which covered a multitude of reasons was 'one on, one here, and one at the wash, Sir'), vests, battledress blouse and trousers and a duplicate set in denim for fatigues, forage cap, gaiters, boots, webbing belt with cross straps and ammunition pouches, groundsheet, blankets, to say nothing of many other odds and ends from brush and comb to shaving tackle.

There was one article of clothing which fortunately was never used for the purpose for which it was intended but became instead one of the most useful things the soldier ever had the good luck to acquire. This was a long voluminous oilskin coat complete with hood attached and with sleeves nicely caught by elastic at the wrists. It was light, easy to roll, and had a fetching mottle for camouflage. It was meant to be a gas cape to protect one's skin and clothing against mustard gas but was universally adopted as a groundsheet-cum-raincoat which offered superb protection against the cold, the rain, and the snow.

So there you have just a little insight into the silly kind of things which originally conditioned the attitude and minds of the hundred of thousands of soldiers who marched into Sicily and Italy in 1943 by way of the western deserts of North Africa on one side and of Tunisia on the other.

For my part suffice to say that I was lucky enough to be selected for a commission in the Middlesex Regiment. I was posted to the 1st Battalion Princess Louise's Kensington Regiment, the Territorial Army protégé of the Middlesex which reformed after losing two companies in the retreat from Dunkirk and then marched proudly with the British Eighth Army into Sicily and Italy too.

3. 'The Jerries won't stand and fight'

'The Jerries won't stand and fight,
they move and fight damn them.'

COMMANDER OF BRITISH DIVISION 1944

Everyone knows that if one looks at a map of the Mediterranean the shape of Italy is like a long elegantly heeled boot with a sharp toe kicking apparently a misshapen football called Sicily. But what few people realise is that this long boot for almost its entire length is stuffed with mountains.

This fact must be emphasised, because the massive Apennines were like a spine which held together the flesh blood and bone of the entire Italian Campaign. From them sprung great ribs of rivers and ravines running in parallel from the centre to the east and from the centre to the west. Nature could have provided no better defensive system designed to hold off any invader moving either way on a north-south axis.

The Apennines are about eight hundred miles in length. In some places they attain a height of nearly ten thousand feet. Over large tracts they broaden out into parallel chains of mountains and plateaux. They are crossed by thirteen principal passes, many of which were established in the first place as Roman roads. Along the coastal plains there are many areas where the gap between the sea and the mountains is very narrow, and where it is broad more often than not there are sizeable foothills which dominate the beaches and the valleys leading into the central range.

It will be appreciated therefore that the presence of these vast obstacles not only constituted a major consideration in every battle but their by-product in terms of meteorology was crucial. They produced the cloud formations which were the harbingers of prolonged torrential rains. They were covered in snow in winter. Drifts and avalanches of giant proportions were commonplace. With the slightest thaw the mountain streams became swollen within the hour. Thus the main river outlets to the sea fed by their gushing tributaries were subject to violent flooding which could raise water levels quite suddenly by as much as twenty feet or more.

In December 1943, when the Eighth Army was engaged in bitter fighting to cross the River Sangro which flows into the Adriatic about two hundred miles north of the heel of Italy, there was an unseasonal thaw in the mountains which combined with heavy rains caused the river to rise dramatically. Bridges built laboriously under shellfire and appalling conditions by the gallant 'sappers' were washed away near the mouth of the river in a matter of minutes. Far from sympathising with his staff concerned, General Montgomery is alleged to have reprimanded at least one of them for not anticipating the problem which he said could have been learnt from any school atlas.

The Germans built strong defensive lines on the high ground over-looking each river. They were very good at it and as they withdrew they got better and better. The American Fifth Army advancing up the west coast of Italy and the British Eighth Army moving along the Adriatic side found the same heartbreak and horror every ten miles as they in turn attempted each crossing and tried to dislodge the well prepared enemy.

The same pattern of this warfare of attrition was to be repeated over and over again. Invariably the bridges were blown up and the first job was to ferry patrols across under cover of darkness to probe the enemy positions, to search for minefields, and to establish a bridgehead if possible so that the Sappers could push a Bailey bridge over the gap in the one that had been blown, or at some convenient point nearby on pontoons. All this had to be done by troops who were already exhausted, who had to work in terrain which was familiar exclusively to the enemy, in pitch-black darkness, and as often as not in pouring rain. In addition enemy fighting patrols, counter-attacks, and well directed fire from mobile guns and mortars, all aimed at the spots which he knew well in advance were the most likely crossing places, caused mayhem. It was a recurrent nightmare.

The wider the water the greater were the odds in favour of the defence and the Germans prepared many months in advance to fortify the major rivers accordingly. They had recruited large work forces from the Todt organisation and local population for this purpose. Observation posts, gun emplacements, vast minefields, machine-gun nests galore, food, fuel and ammunition dumps were all skilfully sited,

protected, and camouflaged. In addition, a host of minor ploys calculated to cause disruption and death ranging from trip wires and booby
traps to individual snipers were used extensively.

The build up of these fortifications became so formidable all along
the length of Italy that like the Maginot and Siegfried Lines the
Germans gave them formal names such as the Winter Line, Gustav
Line, Hitler Line and Gothic Line. The larger rivers became the
settings for great set-piece attacks and bloody battles which lasted for
weeks on end, sometimes months. That is why their names are now
picked out as battle honours on the colours of countless American and
British regiments. The sibilant and musical intonation of so many of
them belie the bitterness with which they are enshrined. Ask any soldier
from any of the thirty nations on both sides who saw service in Italy
if he can identify the Sangro, the Volturno, the Garigliano, the Trigno,
the Moro, the Liri, the Rapido, the Melfa, the Sacco, the Pescara,
the Chienti, the Arno, the Cesaro, the Metauro, to name but a few,
he will recall most if not all of them.

Strangely enough the two most obvious ones, the important ones
mentioned in geography primers, the Tiber and the mighty Po, will
not readily spring to his mind at all. The former for much of its
length runs parallel to the coast and therefore was largely not defended
nor fought over. The latter, the biggest of them all, was a chimera, the
awesome prospect of which he was determined to push from his
consciousness.

The next stage of the river crossing after the establishment of the
grimly held bridgehead came on the completion of the bridge itself.
This enabled tanks as well as essential supplies to get over and the
plight of the surviving infantrymen became correspondingly improved.
Then followed reinforcements, more tanks, more supporting weapons,
until the position was secure. Usually at this point a sort of stalemate
would ensue with each side knocking hell out of the other with a
variety of bombardments from artillery, mortars, and from the air –
an element in which fortunately the Allies ultimately gained great
superiority. It was a short-lived pause which just allowed letters and
hot stew to be ferried forward, for socks and boots to be dried out, for
tea to be brewed, for personal kit and equipment to be checked, for
casualty lists of those killed, wounded, missing and just plain sick to
be established, and above all for what laughingly passed as 'rest' to be
enjoyed.

Young soldiers living for days in the open and pushed to the extremes
of fatigue did not have much difficulty in nodding off in any spare

moments they had, even if they were only propped up against a farm-house wall wrapped in cold wet blankets. The snag was that no sooner had one dropped into oblivion than within a few minutes, or at the most within a couple of hours or so, something always happened to shock one back into the most miserable consciousness. It could be the ear-shattering explosion of a mine, shell, or mortar bomb nearby. It could be the staccato crackle of rifle or machine-gun fire getting closer. It could be the persistent buzz of the field telephone as a signaller sought a response to test a mended line. It usually was in fact the sentry coming off duty, giving one a violent shake because it was time for his relief.

While the comparatively uneventful hiatus was being enacted, the awful routine of patrol duty followed by more patrol duty, both by day and by night, continued incessantly. The infantryman on whom all success depended at every stage of every battle was never allowed, once he was committed, to have any rest at all. It did not matter a damn how sick or tired he felt, if he had any life left in him and was capable of shoving one leaden foot in front of another at less than one minute intervals, he had to take his turn. It would be difficult to find any more frightening and soul-destroying activity of the individual, than going on patrol, especially at night.

Sorties of this nature came in all sorts of fascinating shapes and sizes, according to the men available, their condition, and the kind of information which was being sought. Their whole object was to get information. You could bet your bottom dollar that no sooner had the infantrymen reached his battle objective, than within a matter of minutes, some insensitive commander at company, battalion, brigade, divisional, or even corps Headquarters, wanted patrols to go out to perform some impossibly heroic tasks when the men involved were virtually stretcher cases and should have been wrapped up in warm cosy beds sipping their hot Bovril.

There was the two or three man patrol which went out stealthily just to listen. If they heard the enemy moving about or talking, then this could pinpoint an enemy forward position to be registered at some HQ in due course by a blob on a talc-covered map, for which a china-graph pencil was used, or even by a pin.

There was a patrol ranging in numbers from section to platoon strength, which might be required for a variety of more active assignments, such as reconnoitring possible paths for the next attack, checking out the boundaries of enemy minefields, provoking retaliatory fire so that the enemy would reveal new positions and confirm existing ones, or just for the rather prosaic and ironic function of giving the enemy a sleepless night, and in so doing, imposing the same maddening frustration on oneself.

There was also the 'fighting' patrol, so called because, unlike the others, it deliberately went out to attack and overrun a specially selected enemy position with a view to causing a diversion for an attack elsewhere or to the capture of prisoners. The latter would then be hurried back for interrogation which usually allowed our intelligence officers to make shrewd judgements about the movement of enemy formations, and about their equipment and morale.

It was during the battle of the River Sangro that the horrors of one of these fighting patrols was brought home to me. It was pouring rods of rain and I sought shelter in a partially demolished farmhouse just behind the escarpment overlooking the dreaded river. Beyond the river was a flat morass flanked with paths which ran for about half a mile before lifting into a series of steep cliffs. At the bottom of these our troops were dug in and on top, sitting pretty, were the enemy.

As I stumbled through the entrance I could see in the dim light of dusk a group of soldiers putting on equipment, blackening their faces and tying bits of cloth around ammunition clips and anything which might jingle or make a noise. A match flickered as someone lit a cigarette, and I could not believe my eyes because the face it illuminated was so like that of Terence, a friend I had not seen for four years when we were at school together.

I stumbled forward yet again over packs and sleeping bodies; 'Is that you, Terence?' I asked.

'I'm Terence all right,' he said, 'but who the hell are you?' He lit another match and peered into my face. 'Good God, it's Emily,' he announced.

Our reunion was complete. At our male-dominated school there was one redoubtable lady who had been imported to teach French and her name was Emily Harper. Despite the fact that it differed in spelling, admittedly only in one letter, from my surname, it was naturally pronounced the same and Terence had dubbed me 'Emily' as a result.

In a matter of minutes we had brought each other up to date about our respective careers since we left school. He had joined the Royal Engineers and unknowingly we had been fighting side by side more or less right through Sicily and Italy. It was a joyous happy moment with each basking in a surge of comradeship and nostalgia.

'We're going out shortly,' he said, 'to winkle out a Jerry or two. I've been attached with a few of my chaps to pave the way.'

I could see now in the gloom, as the rain cascaded down on the old tiled roof, that this was a sizeable fighting patrol. 'What do you mean "pave the way"?' and before he could answer I added, 'the only time you paved the way was when you burst out of a scrum in a rugby match at school and passed the ball back to me. The snag was it went so high that it whistled over my head and landed on the referee's whistle which happened to be in his mouth at the time.'

We both burst out laughing. His eyes lit up and he remembered the incident. 'Well, I'll tell you,' he confided. 'We are going through a suspected minefield and I may have to lift a few.'

God, how awful, I thought. Here was one of the nicest, most innocuous, most decent of chaps who at school was voted unanimously to be the one least likely to say 'boo' to the proverbial goose going out into the unknown, to ford a raging river under shell-fire, and then alternately run and crawl his way forward through blinding rain and up to his thighs in icy mud. This agony had to be endured merely to reach our forward positions. It was only the curtain-raiser.

Once having reformed, Terence and the patrol would then start the serious stuff, edging forward on a compass bearing into the darkness over treacherous ground where no friendly foot had trod before and never knowing when a mine would go up, or the enemy would ambush them, or shell or mortar fire would descend upon them. The wind, the rain, the blackness all there to confound them would equally be their allies shielding their movements and dulling any sounds they might make.

The job Terence would then have would be ghastly. As often as not the primitive mine detectors, those instruments which looked like large plates turned upside down and attached to long handles, could only be used for limited sweeps. In the pitch-black night it would be difficult to see what and where one was sweeping and even maintaining a regular height close enough to the ground for the detector to pick up accurate echoes was a problem in itself. The alternative would be to push forward gently on hands and knees and prod the ground somewhat delicately with a spike or a bayonet hoping to hell that if one struck a mine it was not at a sensitive contact point that would set it off.

It requires little imagination to sense the sweating fear of those engaged in this premeditated piece of courage. But this nerve-racking business drawn out over hours of fierce concentration did not simply end with the discovery of a mine. As soon as one's implement made contact the prodding had to go on to establish its shape and its depth under the soil. One's cold and often senseless fingers had to be inserted gently in the crevices to feel for wires, because it was not unknown for the lifting of one mine to set off another attached to it underneath. Meanwhile, the patrol would be creeping forward in a series of irregular movements as silent nods, jerks on equipment, and grippings of arms, and an occasional whisper, indicated directions and the all clear to proceed from one point to the next.

When the patrol had got sufficiently close to their objective for the final assault, the patrol commander would have to make the agonising decision as to where the objective really was, the amount of time he had to do the job and find his way back, and the number of men at his disposal. There is no denying the fact that during the approach a number of men nearly always get lost either by accident and let us face it, by design, and who can blame them? Those who had lost their nerve would mostly turn up later back in their own lines at some opportune moment when the assault was over and a few, surprisingly few, would desert.

And so over a period of hours the nightmare of fear and sweat would be endured to reach the enemy's forward defended localities, or 'FDL's' as they were abbreviated in the army text books. At this point whether or not success attended their attack carried out either silently or with a flurry of exploding hand grenades and light machine-gun and rifle fire, the patrol would only have come half way. The other half would be worse because they would have to find their way back once again over unfamiliar ground with the additional horrors of penetrating both new minefields and lethal curtains of mortar, artillery and machine gunfire all brought to bear on their only lines of retreat as part of a premeditated and well-rehearsed plan by the vigilant enemy in anticipation of precisely this kind of patrol activity.

All these thoughts passed through my mind as I looked at Terence with a mixture of sadness and awe. I knew that his chances of survival were not good. Despite his quiet conversational blandness I knew that he knew that too. Suddenly I felt lonely and sick and sensed that this was in some measure a small sympathetic reflex to the gut-searing apprehension which he himself must have been feeling.

'I've got to push on,' I said abruptly. 'Let's meet up again tomorrow when you get back and have a tot of rum together.'

I described to him how he could find me while we pored over my map to pinpoint the position by the twitching flame of my cigarette lighter. We shook hands in silence.

'Good luck,' I said.

We smiled wanly at each other and I departed with immense foreboding and melancholy.

The next day I learnt that they found the shattered body of Terence in a slit trench. He had been in the process of lifting a mine in open ground when he was caught by some mortar fire which the enemy had the habit of putting down at irregular intervals just to harass our own positions. He had jumped into a slit-trench which appeared miraculously at hand for his protection. What he did not know was that it had been recently vacated by the enemy who had booby-trapped it by placing a mine at the bottom.

When I heard the news I crept miserably away to my hole in the ground which constituted my private quarters at that time and thought of Terence. I knew I should be dwelling on the sadness and injustice of his death and the ghastly futility of war. Instead I found myself saying with fervour the same old prayer I offered every day of the war to the Almighty which for selfish self interest and self preservation could not be beaten. It was 'Oh, please God, don't let me be killed.'

And so the period of stalemate during which the enemy patrols were equally evident was enacted. The hideous chess game of move and counter-move with the private soldiers and patrols providing an unending supply of pawns was played to a point where at last a big set-piece attack could be made. Orders percolated down from army to corps, from corps to division, from division to brigade, from brigade to battalion, from battalion to company, from company to platoon, from platoon to section, from section to poor old, wet, shivering, dirty but indomitable Thomas Atkins – who would have much preferred a pair of dry socks or an extra blanket or, best of all, a letter from home. The trouble about the refinement of orders at each stage of their descent whereby the subordinate recipient was told only what he needed to know was that Thomas Atkins had little opportunity of sharing in the Grand Design. It was all right for the Prime Minister to tell Alexander that his objective was to capture the whole of Italy, which was translated into the 15th Army Group telling the Fifth and Eighth Armies to destroy all enemy forces south of Rome, which in turn determined vast mountain ranges and rivers as key objectives for various corps, but by the time it got down to platoon level the objective had narrowed to one single farmhouse. The difficulty here was that while Tommy Atkins might be aware that something of a world shattering nature was being planned, when it was explained to him that his part in the capture of the farmhouse had been reduced to covering one window or creeping up on the enemy latrine at the back it was not surprising that he was not as excited about the project as the General Staff.

However, it did not take long for one, regardless of rank, to identify the imminence of a major assault by the visible evidence which escalated usually in a matter of days. It was impossible not to be aware of officers coming and going at all sorts of different HQs as they received briefings and orders. Brigadiers and generals could be observed crawling up to forward observation posts in the most undignified manner to have what still stands in the vernacular of the Services as a 'look-see'. Great dumps of petrol, ammunition, shells, bombs and rations would mushroom mysteriously in well-camouflaged bays off the main roads and tracks. There would be an increase in wireless traffic, meaning that more and more messages were being passed backwards and forwards and sideways between units as the preparations mounted and more co-ordination became obligatory. Finally, the troops much to their astonishment and sometimes to their gratification would find themselves pulled out of the line and despatched to a rear area for a few days rest which some-times included a shower in warm water provided by a mobile bath unit. Unfortunately this could be accompanied by the irksome reassertion of certain disciplines connected with cleaning equipment, routine sentry duty, the inevitable kit inspection, and rehearsals of river crossings which did little to sustain any belief that the future could be all that promising.

Then came the great moment for the attack to go in, but not before the forward troops were engulfed by what were called 'Special Orders of the Day'. These were long messages of encouragement and exhorta-tion which each commander added to in turn in the fond belief that when Tommy Atkins got them it would inspire him to perform prodigious feats and to kill at least one extra German which, without this deluge of paper, he would not have been moved so to do. The turgid jargon of these communiqués was often enlivened by a sporting cliché calculated to demonstrate that the Commander had the common touch. For example, General Montgomery could rarely resist the inclusion of some cricketing metaphor such as 'We will hit the enemy for six' or 'I am confident of total victory. The enemy will be caught and bowled before he can run.' Corps, divisional, and brigade com-manders all subscribed their own individual interpretations of what constituted a motivational phrase. 'We have got the enemy on the ropes. This is our chance to deliver the knock-out blow' was one which I recall being used by commanders at different levels for no less than three successive attacks. Naturally this tended to be a trifle counter-productive because, apart from a certain lack of originality which one hoped had not characterised the planning of the authors, it reminded us that as the enemy was still undoubtedly there one must be fighting somebody closely resembling Muhammad Ali.

Another phrase I savoured was used by a brigadier who in passing on the messages from three higher commanders, as he had been ordered to do, added something like 'Never have we been so well prepared for the battle that lies ahead of us. Nothing has been left to chance. God Almighty is assuredly with us. I repeat nothing has been left to chance.' Then, owing to an unfortunate typing error which belied somewhat this infallibility, he signed off with 'Good muck to you all.' It is a matter for speculation that, if the vagaries of fate had induced the errant typist to hit upon another well-known four letter word, then the sex-starved troops might have produced results far exceeding the brigadier's wildest expectations.

It was customary in the interests of brevity and security to give such an operation a code name. The choice of name was not so easy as it might seem because great care had to be taken to avoid one which even remotely suggested the nature or significance of the exercise. For example, on one occasion a Royal Signals detachment listening in on the wavelengths used by the enemy picked up a word in German which was often repeated and which when translated meant 'autumn mist'. It was reported to our Intelligence who concluded (rightly it so happens) that this was a code name for a withdrawal by night under cover of the natural fog rising from low ground at that time of year. As a result we made it a priority to harass their likely lines of retreat with machine-gun, mortar, and artillery fire at appropriate times which must have done much to increase both the tempo and discomfort of this manoeuvre. The only code name I recall which remotely gave our game away to the enemy was one used for an attack on Cassino. It was 'Bradman'. Why the name of that great Australian cricketer should have been picked I do not know, but it is just conceivable that some German with both a sense of humour and some knowledge of British sporting parlance might have detected an echo of Montgomery's 'hit them for six' and have deduced that an onslaught was imminent.

There were two components in the Master plan which had to be left to the last before being specified. One was the actual date of the attack which was known simply as 'D-Day', and the other was the actual hour known as 'H-Hour'. Consequently the outlines of the plan always included pithy references such as 'D−1' or 'D+2' meaning that twenty-four hours before or forty-eight hours after the operation started respectively, certain things had to be done. Although the vicissitudes which beset complicated planning through human error made this advisable, the major consideration in leaving these two vital decisions to the end was the weather. On occasions, even when 'D-Day' had been decided, the time of 'H-Hour' could be in doubt up to the very last moment due to the uncertainty of a meteorological report, or the reality of an unexpected cloudburst.

So at last H-Hour would arrive. More often than not it would be during some period of darkness. As the hands of a host of synchronised watches edged inexorably towards the dreaded deadline, a comparative silence would descend. A nervous, almost sickening, sense of apprehension would seize the regiments of soldiers as they crouched prayerful and tense in ditch and trench. Suddenly an inferno like the crack of doom would burst across the landscape. The overture to the drama about to be enacted would begin with the guns of the Royal Artillery erupting in one heaving salvo on the second of the appointed time.

Then the bombs from the medium and heavy mortars would curve their lethal arc by the hundred. Thousands of bullets from the medium machine-guns beating out their murderous metronome would sweep selected targets on and behind the enemy lines. Great shafts of blinding light would stab the sky as the guns, fed by sweating gunners with ear drums bursting, fired and recoiled. The frightening and unholy noise of staccato, but ever-rolling, thunder assailed one's whole being. Eventually after an eternity when minutes seemed like months, the barrage would lift to enable the infantry to go in behind. The overtone was over. This titanic prelude of terror had raised the curtain.

It was now the turn of the insignificant 'bit' player to be thrust, fearful and unwilling, into the limelight. Tommy Atkins was on. It is a matter of history that he has played his role so well over the centuries, and the excellence of his performance has been taken always so much for granted, that the only rave notice he has ever had is that enshrined posthumously at the Tomb of the Unknown Soldier in Westminster Abbey.

The kind of battle which ensued, both blistering and bloody, will be drawn in greater detail when that which took place for the River Po is described later on. Suffice to say that eventually Tommy Atkins and his allies would fight their way up on to the high ground and, just as they braced themselves for a decisive and climactic coup to overrun the enemy, they would find that there was little or no enemy around to overrun. The Germans were adept at retreating behind the next river obstacle at the psychological moment, the first visible evidence of which would usually be the smoke rising from the bridges they had blown, an affront which seemed uncommonly like that of extending two fingers in a rude gesture to their pursuers.

While attending an 'O' Group, as a meeting of representatives of various sections of the fighting formation was called at which orders were issued, I heard a major-general, no less, explode as he contemplated the frustration and heartbreak of yet another river crossing 'the Jerries won't stand and fight, they *move* and fight damn them'. That just about summed it up, and all the way up Italy the theme song of the troops never strayed far from some variation of 'one more river to cross'.

Time and time again the same pattern would be repeated. Pursue the enemy to the next river and with a bit of luck take a few prisoners on the way. Then would come the nightmare of securing a bridgehead on the other side and the repair of the existing bridge or establishing a new one. This was followed by the patrol chess game ending up in stalemate. The build-up of reinforcements and supplies would ensue as the harbinger of the set piece attack. At last the big battle would start and after nights and days of hand to hand fighting, just as we looked all set to smash the German forces, we would find they had pulled out of the ring in the nick of time and we were back to square one.

One of the things I personally found hard to stomach was the unfair burden of discomfort which was laid upon us, the pursuers. We were always on the move picking our way through minefields and being shelled and mortared and as often as not caught in the open with literally our trousers down. For us there was no happy resting place, no certainty of food and warmth, no security, no recourse to any civilised amenities. The enemy on the other hand retreating to beautifully prepared positions over ground with which he was totally familiar had all of these.

The degree of luxury to which they were accustomed was brought home to me when I explored very cautiously some of the dugouts they had condescended to abandon. These were landscaped like a block of expensive flats and dug deep into a ravine behind the high ground overlooking the river Volturno. I noticed to my disgust that not only did they have every 'mod con' but even the walls were covered with attractive wall paper. I thought to myself, not without some bitterness, that they only needed to put out a few 'FOR SALE' signs when they left, to show their contempt and to ram home the difference in our respective circumstances. I have always felt that the worst thing about the war was the bloody discomfort.

4.   'I'll kill the bastard'

'I'll kill the bastard . . . the bleeding bastard . . .
I'll kill all the bleeding bastards . . .'

INFANTRYMAN AT CASSINO, 1944

The Allied armies tripped on to the mainland at the bottom of Italy in September 1943. They landed virtually unopposed. Yet it was not until April 1945, some nineteen months or more than one and a half years later, that they got to the top, when the great final battle for the River Po took place and the campaign ended.

This works out at a rate of advance of roughly one mile per day. Not very commendable you might think, until you remember that at Cassino alone the Germans did not yield one single yard for more than five months. Consequently it will be clear that the Allies certainly made up for lost time whenever they managed to make a proper break-through. These, alas, were never fully exploited, mainly because the Germans were so adept at withdrawal and then re-grouping.

However, there was one glaring exception where the Allies had the destruction of the opposing armies in the palm of their hand but for, in my view, the excessive over-confidence of one man. He was of such high rank and commanded such political muscle that he got away with it. In my opinion, had he co-operated with the other commanders with the same degree of determination which he had shown in some other matters the war in Italy for all intents and purposes could have been ended nearly a year earlier. In fact it might have been concluded on the eve of the invasion of France in June 1944, thus delivering a shattering blow to the morale of the entire German nation and present-ing Hitler's High Command with the appalling dilemma of either diverting further divisions to try and hold the front in Italy, which were sorely needed for the defence of Western Europe, or allowing the Allied armies to surge forward and attack their 'soft under-belly' from the south via Austria and Yugoslavia. This in turn could well have shortened the war in Europe, let alone in Italy.

When one thinks of the misery and the countless lives that were sacrificed as a result of the prolongation of the campaign one cannot help wondering why the man concerned was not relieved of that command. But it is not as simple as that, and because of my conversations with him years afterwards and putting a lot more than just two and two together I feel, in fact I am certain, that while history may judge him most harshly in the light of this particular episode, it must also in the final assessment of the man concede his qualities as an exceptionally fine commander, a great leader, and as the architect of that textbook battle for the River Po, where because he had learnt his lesson he did not let the enemy get away ever again to fight another day. That man was General Mark Clark.

In a later chapter which I have devoted to him I will tell in more detail the story of this extraordinary event, of its dramatic repercussions, and of the man himself.

As you will now be aware, the pattern of the war in Italy, whenever there was any movement at all, was a *danse macabre* in which the interlocking armies demonstrated not so much the fluid continuity of the quick-step as the slow-slow-quick-quick slow of the fox-trot, which was performed laboriously and with very heavy breathing. There were three distinct intervals when no dancing was allowed because they developed into a static death struggle with, at times, the outcome finely balanced between success and failure on both sides. It is important to mention them briefly because of their effect upon the commanders and their respective armies in subsequent battles in general and the final battle in particular.

The first was at Salerno. If you imagine that the page in front of you is the map of Italy, Salerno is about quarter of the way up on the left hand edge. When the Allied armies crossed over the Straits of Messina from Sicily and landed on the tip of the toe of Italy while near simultaneous landings were taking place around Taranto at the top of the heel in the instep, it was planned to disembark a combined British and American task force comprising several divisions with the help of the Royal Navy on the beaches of Salerno. This could then be used as a bridgehead from which to accelerate the capture of Naples as it was essential to have a large port in order to handle the massive cargoes needed to supply the Allied armies. The bridgehead could also be used as a springboard to cut off the German units retreating in the face of the Eighth Army landings at Messina and Taranto.

There was terrific argument about the suitability of Salerno for this operation because the snag about the generals was that they usually had such a high regard for their own pet schemes and such a compulsion to plant their own metaphorical thumb print firmly on the papers setting out the appreciation of any given situation, it was virtually impossible to get even reasonable unanimity. It always needed some overriding factor to emerge as a catalyst and to concentrate the mind. In the case of Salerno it was the fact that it had the most suitable beaches for the shallow-bottomed landing craft to use which could just about be supported adequately by our fighter planes based in Sicily.

To cut a long and bitter story short, Salerno was a shambles which only the bravery of the troops and junior commanders coupled with the powerful support of the Navy's heavy guns, together with countless RAF sorties, managed to surmount. The composition of our land forces was roughly half American and half British under the overall command of General Mark Clark who was answerable to General Alexander. The British element was X Corps under the command of Richard McCreery who came under Mark Clark. So here we had a relationship between the three commanders which was duplicated precisely some eighteen months later for the battle of the River Po except that by then they all had moved up one so to speak as Supreme Commander (Alexander), Commander-in-Chief Fifteenth Army Group (Clark) and C-in-C Eighth Army (McCreery).

Amphibious landings of this kind are the trickiest things to organise simply because one has to remember that the last things loaded in the craft have to be first off. Therefore, minute attention to detail is required to ensure the correct priorities. Questions have to be decided like who will land first? What will they need first? Ammunition? If so what kinds of ammunition? What about guns and mortars to support them? At what stage should the food come off, so that the assault troops do not starve? Where do the medical supplies come in? What about the trucks and armoured vehicles and tanks? Do the troops need barbed wire and sandbags? Where do the Sappers come in? Perhaps they should land first to lift mines? Hundreds of questions have to be posed and answered. So one can easily imagine that if in the event some of the landing craft go astray or are sunk by enemy mines or shell-fire or by enemy aircraft, troops and equipment absolutely vital to the success of the operation will be lost irrevocably.

It so happened that in 'Avalanche', which was the code name for the Salerno operation, the landings were achieved in such an uncoordinated fashion that only those in the British sector made reasonable headway. The Germans reacted vigorously and nearly pushed back the Allies into the sea. Things got so bad that it was only the reassuring personal appearance of Alexander in the beachhead in the critical moments that prevented a very dubious plan by Mark Clark being implemented. He wanted to move the American beachhead to the area controlled by the British despite all the congestion, confusion and mayhem which this would have involved. Alexander regarded this as a 'quite impossible suggestion'.

It was a very chastening thought that although the Germans only deployed two divisions and a few other elements it was Alexander's opinion that Avalanche would have been a disaster, but for the fact that our air superiority afforded massive cover under which the soldiers could just hang on and the big naval guns of *Valiant* and *Warspite* were allowed to fire the heaviest shells the Germans ever encountered. This shattering bombardment did much to halt or break up their counter attack.

The landings took place on 9th September 1943, and the crisis was not over until the 16th – a week later. The experience undoubtedly sharpened in some respects the mutual regard of our commanders for each other and also in particular for the German soldiers and for Kesselring. But equally it brought to the surface attitudes and frictions which were to endure for some time and perhaps never wholly eliminated for the rest of the war. Alexander's tactful gesture in giving Mark Clark command of the operation although half of the troops were British and the naval and close air support predominantly so must have troubled him when he realised that there was not the incisive command and control at the top which he expected when he arrived at the beachhead. McCreery was not happy about the way things had been handled either. Mark Clark was not all that happy with McCreery because when things go wrong and you are under pressure it is difficult not to be critical of one's subordinates. In addition, Mark Clark blamed General Montgomery coming up from the south for not pushing forward faster with his Eighth Army to link up with the beachhead. The staff work and general co-operation between the Americans and the British at lower levels, though generally competent, often left much to be desired in terms of warmth, comradeship, and genuine mutual understanding.

However, the Salerno beachhead was eventually consolidated and it is a matter of record as well as of great sadness that some of its major lessons had still not been learned by the time a similar operation was attempted at Anzio some four months later. Perhaps the biggest lesson of all was that, with a manoeuvre involving all three services and one so complicated, so hazardous, and so unpredictable as a large scale amphibious attack has to be, only a commander of the highest calibre and fitness who can assess a situation rapidly, who can take instant decisions, and above all who can exploit success should be entrusted with the initial conduct of the beachhead battle. Mark Clark may or may not have been such a person at Salerno, but, by God, he should have seen to it that he got it right when it became his turn to appoint someone to do the same job at Anzio.

The next interval when the dancing had to stop was for a period from 17th January until 18th May 1944, during which the successive battles for Cassino took place. For one hundred and twenty-two days virtually the whole of the armies in Italy on both sides were drawn into this battleground. Volumes have been written about Cassino, about the bombing of its Benedictine Monastery, and about its final capture by the Poles. The reason it became the cynosure of attention is that by this time the whole of the Allied effort in Italy was concentrated on the capture of Rome. This was the main item in a directive given to Alexander by Eisenhower (who was then the Supreme Allied Commander, Mediterranean) on 8th November 1943.

The only way the armies could go for Rome was through the natural route leading to it from the south which is channelled into the Liri Valley, which is flanked by enormous mountains on both sides. The gateway to it is dominated by the awe inspiring and majestic Monte Cassino with its monastery on top. For a thousand years and more the capture of Rome from the south was regarded as virtually an impossibility because of the fantastic natural defences which guard the Liri Valley. They are a combination of mountains and river barriers set in sequences of obstacles and traps which in scale alone no human beings could ever have devised. Horrendous battles were fought here in 1944, and the awful soul-searing impression which penetrated the mind of every Allied soldier who later survived to fight for the River Po was that if you give the Germans the high ground and rivers they can defend, then your days are numbered. This had been hammered home at every previous river crossing, but at Cassino the moment of truth had truly arrived. It was not, I hasten to add, evidenced by the soldiers going around with doom and gloom written on their faces. Far from it, the dedication and comradeship and sheer bawdy humour of Tommy Atkins helped one to keep one's head up, but in the quiet moments, though few would admit it, there was no person actually committed to do combat who was not now consciously resigned to forfeiting his life.

Literally hundreds of thousands of men were drawn into the vortex of Cassino and those who survived have a personal story to tell. I have two at least which I would like to include, not because they are particularly exceptional but because they are of a nature where I can only attribute my survival to the hand of God, and they are typical of the sort of things which happened more frequently at Cassino than in any other battle.

I was second in command of a support group of medium machine-guns and heavy 4.2 inch mortars at the time, and my job was to rest up by day about a mile behind the line and then bring forward by night right up to the front the countless things from sandbags to socks, from bullets to bombs, from cigarettes to bootlaces, which were needed to keep the troops in action.

One day one of my platoon commanders who had an eye for a good bargain reported to me that an American unit wanted to trade a jeep for some whisky. Now a jeep at this time was like gold. This sturdy small four-wheel-drive four seater motor vehicle was a phenomenon in the war. It could do things and go places like nobody's business. It was ideal for ferrying supplies backwards and forwards. I could not believe our good luck.

Suddenly a tinge of justifiable suspicion crossed my mind. 'A jeep is worth a damn sight more than a bottle of whisky,' I said. 'What's the snag?'

'There's nothing wrong with it,' he replied, 'except that it has some sort of jinx. Honestly, I've seen it and it seems quite sound but our American friends are desperate for whisky and they say this jeep just brings them nothing but bad luck.'

I turned this extraordinary and tempting proposition over in my mind. 'What kind of bad luck do they mean?' I asked.

My platoon commander shrugged his shoulders. 'I really don't know,' he said. 'When I pressed them they were very non-committal but I'm sure we can do a deal if we do it quickly.'

It so happened I had several bottles of whisky in reserve as the result of a little prudent housekeeping following previous issues of NAAFI comforts. 'OK let us take a chance. It's too good to miss.'

So off he went and within a matter of hours he returned with what appeared to be a perfectly good jeep. It all seemed too good to be true.

That night in somewhat jubilant vein I and my driver went forward with supplies in our new acquisition to one of our outposts using a track which had been made by our engineers. It was darker than usual as heavy scudding clouds only allowed an occasional glimpse of the clear starlit skies beyond. A fresh wind set my face tingling, and I bent forward against it with head turned to one side to try and make sure I had a good ear to alert me and my driver to the warning 'swoosh' of shell or mortar bomb. One of the hazards of this routine journey to be endured nightly was the spasmodic and often violent harassing fire put down on our supply routes by the inconsiderate enemy.

We started to pass a company of infantrymen also moving forward. One of the men suddenly broke ranks immediately in front of us and started screaming, 'I can't go on, I can't go on.' It was the hysterical cry of a man who had lost his nerve. God knows how many times he had been in and out of the line during the inferno of Cassino, and God knows how many times he must have felt it to be his last. Some could cope better than others and it was only discipline and the firm incisive leadership of the junior commanders who could prevent those drained of their moral fibre from defecting.

I heard the platoon sergeant smacking him in the face to bring him to his senses. 'Get back into line,' he commanded. 'You bloody little man, you are not going to get away with this and leave your mates in the lurch'.

The man, moaning and sobbing, turned back but suddenly broke away again and disappeared into the darkness before a hand could be laid on him. The marching column went stolidly on.

Suddenly I was aware of our jeep being rammed. I was flung forward and upwards out of my seat. My right leg received a crushing blow on the edge of the dashboard just below the knee. I managed to struggle out quite dazed and in great pain. We had been hit head on by an armoured car coming back in the opposite direction. The jeep was virtually a write-off. Fortunately, my driver had miraculously escaped any serious injury, so I told him to stay with the vehicle while I went back for assistance. I set off on what was about a two mile walk, only to find that my progress was extremely painful. My leg, streaming with blood, was throbbing and starting to swell. It was difficult to see and I found myself stumbling in and out of holes and ditches. Then it started to rain.

I struggled on at a slower and slower pace feeling very wet, hungry, and sorry for myself. I had started to despair of getting back to base at all when I became aware of the sound of disjointed words being sobbed out and carried fitfully on the soughing wind which blew from behind me.

'I'll kill the bastard . . . the bleeding bastard . . . I'll kill all the bleeding bastards . . .' I realised it was the poor miserable soldier who had broken ranks earlier who was now following me. I turned around and caught a glimpse of his silhouette when the scudding clouds lifted momentarily. He was perhaps thirty yards away and seemed to be weaving from one side of the track to the other brandishing a rifle. His demented voice was again carried to me: 'I'll kill the bastards . . . all the bastards . . . kill . . . bastards . . . kill.'

In a blinding flash I realised it was my duty to stop and to allow him to catch up with me so that I could apprehend and disarm him. Also in the same blinding flash I appreciated that in so doing I stood the distinct danger of being shot for my pains, an alternative which tended to be more persuasive by virtue of the fact that I was both unarmed and physically incapacitated.

My subconscious and more cowardly instinct made up my mind for me and fear gave me wings. I stumped down the road as fast as I could, determined not to let the confrontation arise. I heard his maniacal murmurs grow fainter. A great relief surged through me and an hour later I stumbled into my bivouac and lay down rigid with cold and pain.

Two days later I was lifted by my batman and driver into the front seat of my truck to go in convoy to another sector on the Cassino front. My leg by this time was not only swollen but had taken on an attractive purple discoloration like that of a squashed dark grape. Every movement was agony. I should have been sent back to hospital but managed to avoid this by enjoining my personal staff to secrecy and by conducting cheerful conversations on my field telephone which suggested I had just had a slight accident and I would soon be as right as rain, and there was an awful lot of rain in Italy to be right about. The reason for my obstinacy in not going back as a casualty was not a brave one. It was simply because I did not want to be separated from my regiment. It was well known that once one got enmeshed in the efficient casualty clearance procedure of the Royal Army Medical Corps not only could one be divorced from one's unit for a long time, but worse still, very often after convalescence one was posted back to a completely different unit, a fate which I viewed with horror.

So, strapped into my seat and with my leg encased in an impromptu splint and bandages, we set off cautiously. My driver did his best to avoid the potholes as he knew the slightest jolt gave me pain. Very soon we caught up with some other vehicles in front and those behind caught up with us. We were in a jam. God, I thought, suppose the enemy start shelling us now. We were always taught to move in convoy with plenty of space between vehicles to avoid excessive casualties in case of enemy fire. Here we had a situation where dozens of vehicles and men were packed along a narrow road together. Fortunately we were in the lee of a steep hill and therefore not under direct observation but the danger of harassing fire was acute in this particular area.

No sooner had I given silent voice to my fear than it happened. There was a 'swoosh' as a shell exploded near a vehicle about seventy yards in front. Instinctively my driver and my batman and I ducked down simultaneously. I realised to my horror that I was not ducking at all. The manner in which I was strapped into my seat coupled with the fixing of my leg into a crevice between the dashboard and axle casing prevented me from doing more than nodding my head.

My driver and batman jumped down and came round to my side. 'Come on, sir,' coaxed my batman who was as dimunitive as his heart was big, 'let's get you out of there and we'll take cover.'

Before he could even fumble with the canvas screen which served as the nearside door of the truck there was another 'swoosh' and a shell burst about a hundred yards behind us. They both hit the ground with the speed born of long practice and instinct. I managed my nod once again.

A cold fear transfixed me. I started to sweat. 'We are being bracketed,' I thought to myself. This is the process in gunnery when you fire a ranging round which falls short of your target and another which goes beyond it, then you can adjust the range more accurately to ensure that the next one hits plumb centre.

My two heroic companions jumped up. 'Come on,' said my batman firmly, now even more aware of my exposed position, 'we'll soon get you out of here.'

I knew that by the time they had struggled to lift me off the truck, in all probability the next shell or two, or even more, would be bursting all around us. Therefore, it was entirely logical that instead of three of us being killed out in the open it was more sensible for those who could take cover quickly to do so.

'Now leave me and take cover,' I said.

They hesitated. Their eyes met mine. I could see their concern for me starting to override their own thoughts of self-preservation. They started to fiddle with the canvas screen.

'Get the hell out of here,' I bawled at the top of my voice, 'go on get the hell out of here.' Then in a quiet tone I enunciated with great deliberation : *'That . . . is . . . an . . . order.'*

My batman looked at me, and as if to combine a gesture of comfort to me and an excuse for his temporary absence he replied with equal deliberation, 'I . . . will . . . bring . . . you . . . some . . . tea, sir.'

Within seconds of their disappearance there was an ear-splitting explosion just down an incline to my left. A shell had burst about twenty yards from my truck but at such an angle that the blast was carried down the slope. At the same time a shell hit the bank about five yards above me. It buried itself deep into the the ground showering me and the truck with great clods of earth. Instinctively I twisted my body away. My heart was pounding. This was it. But I was no more than a bit shocked and dazed, and conscious of the fact that I was still alive.

The silence that followed was first broken by Private J. C. Flynn who hailed from Dagenham appearing like a mirage out of the dust by my side with a mug of tea in his hand. Like the good batman he was, he had made the brew before we had set off and kept it warm in an insulated container which the army had thoughtfully provided for the ferrying of hot stew. I took the mug gratefully and as I sipped the warm sweet liquid I pondered on the fact that nobody but nobody who was as close to a shell as that and in such an exposed position as mine could fail to be killed. Yet here I was sitting up and taking nourishment.

Suddenly it dawned on me. Although it churned up the ground and made things a little unpleasant, the one shell which should have most certainly killed me had failed to go off.

My batman who may have been reading my thoughts said, 'Lucky for us, sir, it was a dud.'

I asked myself why it was that when all the other shells dispensed their lethal explosions quite normally, this one which appeared to have my name on it was the exception. I offered a silent prayer of thanks. A minute or two later I heard the engines of the trucks in front start up and soon the convoy was on its way. After half an hour we arrived safely in the shady olive groves of San Michele, a tiny village a few miles from Cassino.

The second incident occurred after I had been at San Michele for a couple of weeks and my leg had improved sufficiently to enable me to move round on my own again. This was the area from which supplies were sent up to the troops in and around Cassino by night both by mule trains and small jeep convoys. Each time this journey lasting five to six hours for the round trip was a nightmare. The Germans put down immense 'stonks', as the heavy harassing fire was called, almost continuously along all the routes. There was one strip of cratered road in full view of the enemy by day and under his carefully almost lovingly registered shell and mortar fire by night which had to be used by the jeeps. It was called the 'Mad Mile'. Once one got on to it one did not stop. One pressed the accelerator and with head well down one took one's chance with the 'stonks'. Many never made it but it is quite extraordinary the number who did. I for one made a number of these journeys and bore a charmed life.

My last journey was unforgettable if only because it took place on 16th April 1944, my birthday. The medium machine-guns and heavy mortars in my group were in such demand that we had to requisition extra jeeps to carry forward the ammunition to keep them supplied. We also had to carry rations, water-cans, mail, bundles of laundry (yes, we were well enough organised to have a regular exchange of clean clothes for dirty clothes), rum, repaired boots, machine-gun barrels, spare base-plates on which the mortars were mounted, additional tea, sugar and powdered milk. They were all sorted out and neatly labelled for easy identification in the dark when we arrived. Three or four men coming back from hospital or from a short spell on leave took their places in the spare seats beside the gallant drivers of the Royal Army Service Corps. Then as dusk fell we assembled in the staging area and I took my seat in the leading jeep. We moved forward to the start-point which was where a number of tracks criss-crossed and dubbed by my Cockneys 'Clapham Junction' in nostalgic memory of that famous railway complex in London. One by one the convoys left at suitable intervals.

Eventually the Military Police called out 'Kensingtons next – off you go'. Not without misgivings I put on my moral armour and prepared to do battle with the terrors of the darkness. Then as if I had some premonition I did something which I did not normally do. I put on my steel helmet as well. Not only that, I put it on very firmly and I adjusted the chin-strap with great care. One may well ask why in a world of shot and shell one did not wear one's steel helmet all the time. The fact was that the steel helmet was heavy and uncomfortable and one adopted a certain philosophy about the risk ratio of wearing it but somehow, such is the quirk of human nature, one does not take readily to doing so. My driver I was glad to note was wearing his, and before I could attach any conscious significance to my unusual gesture to my own self-preservation my mind was occupied with the ritual drama that lay ahead.

The last flicker of natural light behind the brooding Monastery had already been replaced by the staccato flash of exploding shells and bombs as our little convoy pushed forward, twisting and turning along the tortuous track. Suddenly my jeep bounced in and out of a shell-hole and almost shuddered to a standstill. My driver swore and mentally noted the location. That shell-hole had not been there the night before. He and I were now straining in nervy concentration, particularly in the frequent intervals when the jeep had to slow down and the noise of the engine abated to catch the sound of the inevitable shell. We heard a strident whistle of one going overhead and which exploded a couple of hundred yards behind us. This was followed by another and then two more. Instinctively we lowered our heads and the driver stepped on the accelerator steering a miraculous course in degrees of visibility which swung from total darkness to shadowy outlines to momentary clear-cut silhouettes, reflecting the ever changing patterns of light of the inferno of the battlefield.

As we turned into the 'Mad Mile' a string of small red lights, such as those you see on Christmas trees, was curving a graceful arc high above us which slowly melted into the darkening void. It took me a few moments to work out that the Germans were firing tracer bullets, ammunition which had a certain phosphorous element which enabled one to follow it by eye, into Cassino. Flares went up over Monastery Hill and over the big mountain behind it called Monte Cairo, and seemed to hang in the air as if suspended by invisible wires. They threw out enormous light. We pushed on grimly along the cratered road feeling absolutely naked. Just ahead of us was one patch particularly well illuminated by a flare which seemed to be drifting in our direction. We dared not stop as that would hold up the jeeps behind. We knew that if we bunched the danger of severe casualties and loss of supplies would be enormous. In any case if we pulled off the road and tried to take cover we faced the almost certain risk of being blown up on mines which the Germans had littered along the sides and in the ditches. They were too numerous and sited in too exposed positions for the Sappers to be able to clear them.

Suddenly the 'stonk' which we felt must assuredly come, was heralded by the most unnerving noise I personally have ever heard. It was the sound made by the German Nebelwerfers. These were multi-barrelled mortars which sent bombs off in quick succession, each with the frightening screech of a demented banshee. It made the blood go cold and the hair on the back of the neck bristle with apprehension. At night when one was already sick with anxiety and up-tight with just plain terror, the addition of this awful sound and the menace behind it was paralysing. Within seconds the moaning bombs were whining and sobbing overhead and then bursting all around us.

We bent low behind the dashboard but my driver with one half-open eye kept going. The little jeep banging in and out of the holes veered from one side of the road to the other. But for the fact that the ammunition in the back was packed neatly in boxes and cases and tied down securely we would have lost it all by now. We were then forced to churn along in first gear in order to negotiate a difficult patch. Our speed was down to a crawl. I felt sure we would be hit. But no, although the bombs and shells continued to straddle us at intervals we and the rest of our little convoy arrived unscathed at our destination. We unloaded our supplies, exchanged messages and had a smoke. We had been through a tough situation but not much worse than any other night. But now the really awful part was to come. We had to go all the way back again not only with our 'empties' but also carrying the sick and wounded. The 'Mad Mile' was waiting for us.

The return journey was astonishingly quiet. One never knows why such things happen but it was not until we were half way along the 'Mad Mile' that I thought about my steel helmet. I was about to take it off when something made me stay my hand. There appeared to be no unusual enemy activity. No shell nor bomb had disturbed us unduly. The driver was even humming a repetitive phrase of 'Campdown Races'. Before I could analyse my reluctance to discard my headgear there was a loud bang in the air above us. I felt a stunning blow on the side of my head which knocked me unconscious.

When I came to, I found myself sitting in a jeep with a different driver and my steel helmet had a big slice of the rim bent downwards over my right ear. It had saved my life. It appeared that I had been hit by a fragment of shell which had exploded above our heads and I toppled sideways out of my jeep. My driver who was fortunately unharmed did not realise I had vanished until much farther on but by that time the jeep behind me had picked me up.

Here again I was amazingly lucky because the driver of the second jeep spotted me lying on the side of the road by the light of a terrific salvo delivered by our own guns which illuminated the skies and the countryside at the critical moment. Normally he would have ignored a body on the road. One did not hang around for dead bodies. But on this occasion he told me something made him do it. He quickly perceived who I was and that I was uninjured. Apparently I half got to my feet which helped him considerably in bundling me into the seat beside him, although I was not really conscious of what I was doing until we had got nearly back to base.

My battered steel helmet became an object of considerable curiosity and many a visitor beat a path to my bivouac to examine it, not so much because they were interested in my story which I was hard put not to embroider, but because it was visible evidence that the damn thing was worth carrying around after all.

5. 'Time Spent on Reconnaissance'

'Time spent on reconnaissance is seldom wasted unless
you're trying to find a woman in Italy . . .'

FRED MAJDALANY
(in conversation with the author)

The battles in and around Cassino only came to an end after four
months' hand to hand fighting, and then ironically in a manner which
was the reverse of that originally intended. When the Allies were halted,
Alexander planned another amphibious landing like the one at Salerno
at Anzio about sixty miles behind the enemy lines, and close to the main
routes leading into Rome. This thrust would continue inland to cut the
German communications, and it was hoped that such a threat would
force a general withdrawal of the enemy from the whole of their Gustav
Line which had Cassino as its pivot.

On 22nd January 1944 some 50,000 Anglo-American troops under
the command of Major-General John P. Lucas of the United States
Army and some 5,000 vehicles began landing. Within forty-eight hours
most of the troops were ashore, and the first objectives had been
captured without opposition. An advance of seven miles had been made
to the Alban Hills. The high ground they provided was the vital
territory, and with one more quick decisive move by the Allies this
great prize and probably Rome itself would have fallen like a ripe plum
into their hands at virtually no cost. But at this point General Lucas
faltered. He remembered how at Salerno the Germans had nearly
knocked the Allies back into the sea before they could consolidate the
beachhead. So he waited for more tanks and guns to be landed and
ignored the beckoning prize of the high ground which would have won
him the day.

It must be said here that General Mark Clark concurred with his
plan. He liked Lucas and had picked him for the job. However, it is

a matter of record that he was forced to relieve Lucas of his command a month later when the Anzio operation became as badly bogged down as the one at Cassino. Those precious hours which Lucas wasted in being over-cautious enabled the Germans to keep their grip on the Alban Hills and to counterattack with a ferocity that prevented the Americans from ever getting so close to them again, until the Fifth and Eighth Armies broke through the Gustav Line eventually in May and brought much relief to the beleaguered Anzio bubble. Over 30,000 casualties were evacuated from here during the four-month hell on this beachhead and in the end the Gustav Line collapsed as the result of the very type of frontal attack which the landing from the sea at Anzio was designed to avoid.

It was an affair which military critics and historians will debate forever. Churchill was very piqued about it. He had done much to ensure that the fleet of landing craft required to carry such a big force and their equipment had been retained in Italy for this particular operation, despite being earmarked as a matter of urgency for the invasion of France. When he learned of the way things were going he growled to the effect, 'I expected to see a wildcat roaring into the mountains and what do I find? A whale wallowing on the beaches!'

Alexander was upset about the way the conduct of operations had been reported in British newspapers and he thought he could stop bad news appearing by cutting off facilities for correspondents to file stories. When it was pointed out to him that none of the stories of which he had complained came from Anzio he said to the correspondent who had put this point, 'Well if you didn't write them, somebody did, and you'll get no more facilities for wiring from here.'

While Alexander blamed Lucas for the debacle because he was too slow to exploit the advantage which the element of surprise had given to him, he conceded that a month elapsed before he himself could persuade Mark Clark to dispense with Lucas's services. He felt that the whole thing was very much an American affair and it was inappropriate to intervene. He admitted it took an effort of will to confront Mark Clark eventually with even a gentle ultimatum about Mark Clark losing his command before the latter took the necessary action by replacing the unfortunate Lucas with the formidable Major-General Lucius K. Truscott who commanded the Third United States Division in the beachhead.

This relationship between the generals raises an interesting point. If Lucas was to blame for the failure of the operation then the man who picked him for the job, namely Mark Clark, should have been fired first. But then Alexander, who was Mark Clark's immediate superior and who allowed things to drift for a whole month before he 'persuaded' Mark Clark to do palpably what he should have ordered Mark Clark to have done much earlier, is in a way even more to blame. One thing you could say about Field Marshal Montgomery is that if things were not going according to his plan he tore into the senior subordinates concerned, as my story about his reaction to the bridging operation over the River Sangro has testified.

There will always be argument about exactly where the 'buck' stops and the tolerance shown by Alexander towards Mark Clark at this time is somewhat inexplicable. In their respective memoirs each gives the impression of being the victim of circumstances and of being able to do little about it. It was clear to Mark Clark that Lucas was 'tired' right at the beginning yet he was reluctant to switch the command. In essence he chose the wrong man for the job and it was only when he was told, according to Alexander, that he himself faced the sack that he acted. But Alexander's equal reluctance to bring things quickly to a head with Mark Clark and to have it out in the open showed a weakness, if not of character, certainly of judgement on this particular matter.

In fact Alexander's trust in Mark Clark, born partially of his genius for delegating with the minimum interference and of his desire to take account of the political nuances to which the Americans were very sensitive, produced in him a blind spot. This was to have disastrous consequences when Alexander requested a certain assurance from Mark Clark about his future intentions when the break-out from Anzio was at last achieved.

It was in May 1944 that this happened and it occurred not because of the weight of a great offensive launched from within the perimeter, but because the Allied pressure on Cassino and subsequently through the Liri Valley caused the German defences to crumble and their withdrawal almost became a rout. The two main roads which permitted the German armies south of Anzio to be supplied and ultimately to escape could be cut by a decisive thrust eastwards from Anzio itself as long as it was done with the determination and vigour. This would have ensured such destruction of the enemy forces that for all intents and purposes the campaign in Italy could have been brought to a triumphant conclusion a year earlier than it was, and the fall of Rome, the main objective, would have been achieved automatically as a result.

It was abundantly clear to Alexander that the first priority when the enemy started to beat a hasty retreat was to use the Anzio base, so bitterly contested and held, as the God-given means of blocking the enemy's escape. This would destroy him, and Rome and all the other cities for that matter would fall as well. If on the other hand the Allied forces emerging from Anzio went north to capture Rome instead of going east to cut off the enemy's routes, they would certainly capture Rome but the enemy had a good chance of escaping and of living to fight another day. Never was there a more clear-cut and obvious course of action open to our generals. Never was such an opportunity thrown away.

Alexander made his intentions clear. In fact Mark Clark conceded in his own book *Calculated Risk* that Alexander had been adamant that the attack from Anzio should go east to cut off the enemy retreating from Cassino. Why then when the crunch came, and Mark Clark with his very considerable forces was poised to cut off the German retreat from Cassino, did he not do it? One wonders what calculations must have possessed him at that time. Equally one has to ask how Alexander allowed Mark Clark to get away with it, especially in view of his previous experience in dealing with Mark Clark over the General Lucas affair. But first one should have a little more background to this bizarre situation.

In May 1944 when all this was happening, I and my fellow officers knew enough about the general picture to appreciate that it only needed the Anzio beachhead force to punch across the German lines of communication to cut their retreat and inflict not just a heavy blow but perhaps one which would put paid to the war in Italy. Our spirits were high. Having fought over one river after another and watched the enemy beat an orderly retreat to fight yet again another day, we thought it almost too good to be true that at last we had him clearly cornered.

I recall from a brief note in my diary at that time a conversation I had with my immediate superior, Major John Doyle, about one, Bob Edgecombe, who had just been promoted to Quartermaster of our regiment. John said to me in his dry way, 'A pity dear old Bob here will not enjoy his new rank for long.'

'What do you mean?' I asked, somewhat surprised. 'He'll be first class. Don't forget Rocky taught him all he knew.' This was a reference to our beloved Quartermaster Rocky Knight who was regarded as the custodian of all wisdom and knowledge worthwhile in the illegal acquisition of army equipment and rations. He had served for a decade with the regiment before retiring, and also incidentally before being found out.

John looked at me for a second absolutely deadpan and said, 'He'll be lucky if he sees another month's service.' I stiffened with incomprehension. Then John burst out laughing. 'We've got the buggers on the run. With the boys from Anzio cutting them off the war will be over in ten minutes and we'll all be out of a job!'

Although this observation was somewhat nonchalant and facetious the force of John's speculation hit me between the eyes. Up till then I had never thought much more about strategic matters than where a good safe latrine could be dug and where my next meal was coming from. Now the whole simple happy climax of what it was all about beckoned to me. In a blinding flash I grasped the significance of the glittering opportunity which lay literally only a few miles ahead. Here we were surging past Cassino and chasing the whole of the German Tenth Army up two main routes which our Anzio forces could cut at will. We would thus trap and destroy an entire army.

'By God, John,' I said, 'You might be right.'

He looked at me quite seriously as he fingered his moustache reflectively. 'By God, Brian,' he said, 'I might be right.'

That fleeting and somewhat superficial conversation sowed a seed in my mind which drove me over the years to find out what went wrong.

My quest not only led me into a personal confrontation years later with Mark Clark but at the same time it gave me the key which unlocked the explanation about how the battle for the River Po evolved and why it became such an extraordinary affair.

My latent curiosity about the decision of Mark Clark to change the direction of his attack and so let the enemy off the hook was stoked by fortuitous happenings over the years. The first was a chance conversation with Field Marshal Alexander, in a stable of all places, where I was grooming a reluctant horse and this caught his eye. It occurred in March 1945, and I will refer to it later.

Then about 1955 I bumped into Fred Majdalany in Tudor Street, near Fleet Street in London. This was not so surprising because at that time we were both working for the *Daily Mail* to which he made regular and distinguished contributions as the paper's film critic. We had first found out our mutual involvement in Fleet Street when we shared a slimy dug-out behind the ridge overlooking the River Sangro in Italy in November 1943. He was in the Lancashire Fusiliers, was subsequently wounded, and had won the Military Cross. We had met

The author commissioned as 2nd Lieutenant in the Middlesex Regiment 1940

(*Right*) This picture of the anti-tank gun crew of the Jewish Brigade is interesting because the men from left to right represent England, Hungary. Russia, Czechoslovakia, Austria, Palestine, Egypt and Poland.

(*Below*) Soldiers coming out of line for brief rest examine a German Mk 6 Tiger Tank with its 88mm gun. This one was knocked out by an infantryman with a hand-held personal anti-tank weapon called for short a 'PIAT'. It took great courage to get close enough to do this sort of damage.

Heavy mortar platoon of the Kensingtons going into action on the command 'take posts' in northern Apennines, January 1945. By this time they enjoyed the luxury of firm frozen ground and the issue of white duffle coats.

This picture, taken at the collection point before the mules had even started their nightmare journey under cover of darkness, gives some idea of the difficulties they and their gallant muleteers faced. The mule trains like these were operating continuously in the northern Apennines for nearly five months.

Field Marshal Alexander

each other before on various office occasions but had never done much more than exchange a few pleasantries.

This time he invited me to adjourn for a drink in what was known as the 'Mucky Duck'. It was in fact an undistinguished but friendly little pub called the White Swan, which was next door to Northcliffe House, the headquarters of the *Daily Mail*.

'I am collecting material for a book about Cassino; have you anything you can tell me?' he asked. We had fought alongside on several occasions in the shadow of the Monastery and I had already read his book entitled *The Monastery* which was a brilliant first-hand account of the influence this massive and historic building had upon all those whom it dominated in the bloody battles around its base.

'Not another book on Cassino,' I exclaimed. 'Surely this as a subject has been written out?'

'Not so,' he replied tersely. 'The more I go into it the more I find stuff which nobody knows about.' He went on to tell me just a little about new information he had uncovered from reading various papers and diaries about the nature of the operations, and particularly about the reaction of the Germans to the successive assaults of the Allied armies. I was not much help to him but we went on talking and then he said something which stuck in my mind.

'That brooding monastery ate into our souls. You were there and I was there and there was never any doubt in our minds, nor in the minds of anyone else that it had to be bombed. No way could we or anyone else conceive that it was not occupied by those mad German paratroopers and crammed with enemy observation posts.'

I readily conceded it had never occurred to me or anybody else that it was unoccupied by the enemy. That would have been a ridiculous assumption given the enormous advantages to the enemy its occupation conferred, and having regard to our own appreciation of the efficient and ruthless way the enemy had exploited anything in his favour all the way up Italy. As for the malevolent Monastery eating into the soul, I told Fred Majdalany about my attempt to exorcise its influence by my having done a rather inspired but very amateur oil painting of it in 1947 from memory. This had won me third prize in a village competition in Old Windsor for which I received the equivalent of 15p, although I had to confess that my joy in being placed third in the competition with my very first effort in oils was put somewhat into perspective by virtue of the fact that only four entries were submitted for adjudication. It hangs on the wall of my living room to this day and is greatly admired by those who wish to curry favour with me, and by members of my family who know its sentimental value to me.

'What are you going on about the bombing of the Monastery for?' I asked him. 'You are right. Everybody knew the enemy must be there and if no attempt had been made to bomb it we would have assumed that the generals simply did not want any of our attacks to succeed.

'Maj.', as we called him, went on, 'Have you read General Mark Clark's book? Because if you have you will be probably just as sick as I am that he tries to give the impression that he was never in favour of the bombing. Yet he was the man, he was the man,' repeated Maj with quiet emphasis, 'who despite his misgivings gave way to Freyberg and ordered the Monastery to be bombed'.

I told him that I had not read the book. 'Well you should,' he said. 'It's called *Calculated Risk*, and it's a real eye-opener. Not only is our gallant General apparently using a liberal amount of hindsight to justify his actions at every stage by quoting from his diary to prove how right he always was, but one gets the impression that he spent so much time writing his diary for this very purpose that he could not have had any time to fight battles. And another thing,' went on Maj who was by now warming to his subject, 'Mark Clark admits that Alexander told him to cut off the Germans retreating from Cassino by bursting out of Anzio and seizing the main roads. Yet a few days later Mark Clark said was "shocked", yes "shocked" that's the word Mark Clark used,' repeated Maj with his quiet emphasis and adjusting his glasses slightly, 'because Alexander specified the date and direction of this attack without reference to Mark Clark. Dammit, Alexander was the commander-in-chief who had to co-ordinate everything. He told Mark Clark what he wanted to do for days and days beforehand and yet when he gave the signal for the plan to go forward our dear Mark Clark says he was "shocked" that he had not been consulted.' Maj looked at me enquiringly. I could tell he wanted me to ask a question. I thought for a moment with my mind racing back to those fateful days and suddenly I recalled my conversation with John Doyle and General Alexander some ten years earlier.

'I always wondered why we let the buggers get away when they had to pull out of Cassino and the Liri Valley,' I mused out loud. Maj paused and said very quietly: 'I believe it was because that man Mark Clark was so obsessed with taking Rome that he forgot where the enemy was.'

All this re-awakened my interest so much that I never forgot this conversation, which also included another Maj epigram I still treasure.

At one point we were reminiscing about army training and the clichés in the manuals which summarised the message the trainee was meant to get. Because of the importance of studying the ground very carefully over which one had to move, especially if one was going on patrol, there was the oft used phrase 'time spent on reconnaissance is seldom wasted'. I mentioned this to Maj who chewed it over for a few seconds. 'Yes,' he said thoughtfully, 'that's true practically of everything in life.'

By then we were leaving the bar and I asked, 'Can you think of any instance when it doesn't apply?'

Maj without the slightest hesitation said impishly, 'Yes, time spent on reconnaissance is seldom wasted unless you are trying to find a woman in Italy'.

I burst out laughing and we spent another five minutes chatting on the pavement as we recalled the hilarious antics we all got up to in trying to find a woman in Italy. One friend of mine virtually climbed Vesuvius with a gleam in his eye and a tin of bully beef in his hand as bait, in search of anything which would satisfy his sexual desires. The young girls in every town we liberated either went voluntarily or were pushed underground, and those who could be observed on a clear day with powerful binoculars were so heavily chaperoned that nothing less than a frontal attack on the scale of Cassino could prise them away. It was only when one went back to the rest camps or to the major cities well to the rear that one had a hope of having any feminine company. Therefore, it was rare for the front line soldier to be able to translate his sexual fantasies, rendered somewhat obsessive by long abstinence as they were, into reality.

It was in 1957 that Fred Majdalany's wonderful book *Cassino – Portrait of a Battle* was published. It was not until the final chapter he wrote about the extraordinary behaviour of Mark Clark which we had discussed in the 'Mucky Duck'. He refers to the 'astonishing change of plan' when Mark Clark ordered General Truscott to change direction to capture Rome instead, as Alexander had wanted, to keep going for Valmonte, the spot on Route 6 which would cut off the retreat completely of the German Tenth Army. He describes how General Truscott was 'dumbfounded' on being given this order. In fact Truscott said this was definitely not the time to change the plan. Things were going so well that the seizure of Valmonte, the original objective, was at hand and would 'ensure the destruction of the retreating German Army'. Truscott, a great United States general by any criteria, then went on to make a critical assessment as far as Mark Clark was concerned when he said :

'There has never been any doubt in my mind that had General Clark held loyally to General Alexander's instructions, had he not changed the direction of my attack to the north-west on 26th May, the strategic objective of Anzio would have been accomplished in full. To be first in Rome was poor compensation for this lost opportunity.'

In the interim I had read Mark Clark's *Calculated Risk* and I have since pondered long upon the enigma of his apparent success in the face of so many questionable incidents. I recalled how his handling of the Salerno operation did not appear to have commended itself particularly either to Alexander or McCreery. Later the latter, a most experienced and resourceful general, was so utterly opposed to Mark Clark's plans to cross the river Volturno that he had to make an issue of it. He said, 'I am embarrassed when an American gives British troops orders we don't like.' Whatever the merits or demerits of the Mark Clark plan, the fact is that Mark Clark pulled rank, said in effect 'orders are orders' and McCreery, being the good soldier he was, obeyed them. How differently this contrasts with Mark Clark's behaviour when he was faced with the same situation vis-à-vis Alexander in the break-out from Anzio.

Following the Volturno incident there was the questionable decision taken by Mark Clark in January 1944 to force the crossing of the River Rapido near Cassino against the advice of his experienced subordinates. This once again was conceived by him in conjunction with Anzio to accelerate the march of his Fifth Army on Rome. It was common knowledge among many of us at that time that the first crossings of the Rapido by the Americans were an unmitigated disaster. The loss of American lives was horrific. Indeed it reached such proportions that the survivors of the 36th 'Texas' Division which had performed previously with great success until it had been decimated in this battle called after the war for a congressional investigation. They described the operation as 'one of the colossal blunders of the Second World War' and a 'fiasco' and attributed the blame for it to General Mark Clark. It is only fair to point out that when the furore arising from this accusation forced a review of the evidence to be made, the US Secretary of War, at that time Robert P. Patterson, exonerated Mark Clark. But this only stirred up more resentment in Texas and as a result the Committees on Military Affairs of both the US House of Representatives and of the US Senate called for witnesses to give evidence so as to establish if an official congressional investigation was really warranted. General Walker, the Commander of the 36th Division at the time, and others gave their versions which indicated that the plans to cross the Rapido imposed upon them by 'Higher Command' were badly based, lacked judgement, and in short were simply suicidal. There was a hint that some of this was due to the 'West Point Protective Association' (West Point being the well-known US academy which supplies regular army officers like General Mark Clark). This, alleged Colonel Ainsworth, President of the 36th Division's Association, was responsible for allowing officers to assume high command 'regardless of their known ability'. The whole controversy was described later in detail by Martin Blumenson in his excellent book *Bloody River*. It needs to be said once again in fairness to Mark Clark that Blumenson came to the conclusion that what emerged from the hearings was 'no strong case against Clark'. In fact he suggests that with 'more determination and push the crossings [of the Rapido] could well have succeeded'. Nevertheless, it appears that Mark Clark had a knack, to put it mildly, in a number of his major amphibious operations of attracting considerable misfortune and criticism before their ultimate success was realised.

I received a further dramatic reminder of the contentious issues involved when as the General Manager of the *Sunday Dispatch,* a post to which I had only just been appointed, I went down to the machine room one Saturday night in September 1957 to see the first copies being run off. The machine room overseer flicked through a rather inky copy with me and there, as he turned the page, was the bold headline 'Was this the war's biggest blunder?' It was an account of an interview which our splendid correspondent Christopher Lucas, prompted by Fred Majdalany's book, had secured with Mark Clark in the United States. Deliberating on the accusations in the book that Mark Clark had flouted Alexander's orders following the Cassino/Anzio break-out and had failed to cut off and destroy the retreating German forces while opting instead for a full-scale American attack on Rome, Christopher Lucas said :

'I asked Clark bluntly, "Did you disobey Alexander's orders after Cassino?" He answered, 'I know what they say but it is not true" Yet after going point by point through the Italian campaign with Clark for more than two hours I believe the critics are right.'

Such was Lucas' verdict, and I realised that the only way I could resolve the enigma of Mark Clark was to have it out with him myself. How else could I reconcile to my own satisfaction the criticism which

assailed him on all sides for his alleged military blunders and lack of
judgement with his subsequent promotion to command of the 15th
Army Group which he inherited from Alexander, who should have
been least disposed to give it to him? How could a man whose conduct
of operations was on so many occasions at least questioned to become
overnight as it were the 'Supremo' of that remarkable textbook
battle – the battle for the River Po? It was not until seven years after
reading Christopher Lucas' provocative and thoughtful piece in the
Sunday Dispatch that I found out.

All this brought into focus and perspective a conversation I had quite
inadvertently in 1945 with General Alexander as he then was. It took
place a few weeks before the battle for the River Po started. I had
been sent back hundreds of miles from the front to a small town called
Benevento near Caserta, which was the main headquarters of
Alexander's Mediterranean Command, in order to attend a senior
officers' school. This was intended for young officers of what was called
field rank, that is with the title of 'major' upwards, so that they could
be instructed and reported upon with a view to subsequent promotion.
My own interpretation of soldiering was so far removed from the
orthodoxy and conventions of the regular army I suspected I had been
sent there by Laurie Bryar, who was then my kind and understanding
commanding officer, more in the hope that I would simply get a rest
than in the expectation that my military prospects would be improved.

At this school we were given horses to ride, so that we could make
forays into the surrounding countryside where things called TEWT's
were performed. A TEWT was the abbreviation used to signify a
Tactical Exercise without Troops. It enabled one to make appreciations
of situations, to issue orders both verbally and on paper, and to fight
the most ferocious battles without a drop of blood being spilt. It was
in fact a challenge to the imagination which ranked with the same
mind boggling improbability as that which I once described to a group
of my brother officers as a JEWT. This I explained gravely was a
Jungle Exercise without Trees. I was gratified to note that my reputation as a wit rose, albeit momentarily. I had sufficient familiarity with
horses, as a result of my early childhood in Ireland where horses were
regarded at that time as being preferable to the Model T Ford, to know
that it was wise if one could to inspect one's animal beforehand. This
was even more prudent when one considered that the horses used at
the school were tended by German prisoners of war who obviously
relieved their boredom by ensuring that the most recalcitrant and
difficult animals were off-loaded on to the unsuspecting British officers,

many of whom had no closer acquaintance previously with these noble beasts than that provided by a visit to a bookmaker. I had gone to the stable where the horse allocated to me was quartered and was somewhat relieved to find that it was apparently quiet, well-behaved, and had a reasonable mouth.

Fortified with this knowledge I indicated to the German groom that he could leave while I busied myself walking cautiously around my new-found friend and uttering what I imagined to be soothing noises. Suddenly I realised I was not only running my fingers through his mane but was actually brushing him down while singing in a broad Irish accent a snatch of an old Irish song called 'The Wearin' of the Green'. This was an unconscious and spontaneous throw-back to the days when as a little boy of six I used to watch Pat Purcell, our very Irish odd-job man and custodian of the horse which pulled the family trap, as he bedded down the animal for the night. He sang the song in a sort of nasal rhythmic baritone which had a hypnotic effect accompanied as it was by the smell of soft new straw and the dancing shadows cast by the storm lantern against the dappled whitewashed walls.

Overwhelmed by nostalgia my imitation of dear Pat rose in volume until it could be heard well outside the stable precincts. As the words dwelt somewhat upon the eternal injustice inflicted by the English on the Irish anybody passing at that time might well be excused for thinking it was not a British officer serving in His Majesty's Forces for the purpose of fighting His Majesty's enemies, but exactly the reverse.

I had got to that part which said, not without considerable pathos and emotion as I lustily interpreted it, 'and the shamrock is forbid by law to grow on Irish ground' when under the belly of the long suffering animal I saw the most beautifully polished pair of brown riding boots I had ever seen standing on the other side.

I stopped short, raised my head, and peered over the top. It took me several seconds to realise that in those boots was an immaculate officer of high rank, sporting an elegant peak cap and boring into me with the coldest light blue eyes I had ever met.

I snapped to attention like a frenzied mousetrap. I was shocked out of my mind. I recognised General Alexander. There was no mistaking him. He looked exactly like his photograph. My heart thumped. I was dimly conscious of one or two other officers now looking in through the stable door, one of whom resembled strongly the school commandant. They had obviously been escorting the General on an informal visit around the premises before he addressed the students like myself, and he had found himself diverted by my raucous and disembodied voice.

Frankly, I was terrified. It was comparable with the bombing at Cassino. He did not shift his ground nor did he take his eyes off mine. It all seemed too embarrassing somehow. Suddenly his eyes and mouth softened in a slight smile. To me it was like a burst of sunshine erupting from behind a thunder cloud. 'You are Irish and you like horses,' he stated as if it were a mutually supporting glimpse of the obvious. I do not know what possessed me but I had the nerve to smile back and say, 'Yessir, I am Irish, I do like horses, but this is one I am trying to make like me.'

'Oh,' he said, 'is this a case of getting to know your enemy?'

It was a gentle quip calculated to put me at my ease. Indeed I found I was no longer standing to attention as I explained to him that I thought it was a wise precaution to look over the animal which was destined to carry such a precious burden as myself on the next TEWT.

He then went on to ask me what part of Ireland I came from and when he discovered I had gone to school at Portora in Enniskillen in Co Fermanagh in the north of Ireland he reminisced a little about his home in Caledon in the adjoining county of Tyrone. It was obvious he loved the place and we touched upon the fishing on Lough Erne and the lovely walks over countryside we both knew well. All this took but a few minutes and in a way which only mutually shared private knowledge can induce we were chatting in a far more relaxed way than I ever had the right to expect or enjoy.

He went on to ask me about my regiment and where I had seen action. Spotting my divisional 'flash' on the top of my sleeve which was a small square piece of cloth having a yellow battleaxe on a black background he said, 'Ah, I see you are 78th Division. You were with the Fifth Army for a while. Tell me how did you get on with the Americans?'

It was such a surprising question that it took me a second or two to react. Yet it was a natural one because as the two armies the Fifth and the Eighth were composed mainly of American and British troops respectively it was of concern to him as their overall commander about how they co-operated at lower levels like mine.

'Frankly, Sir,' I said, 'I have not had much to do with them but I did have a small detachment of GI's under my wing for about twenty-four hours when we were fighting up in the mountains last October.'

'Were they "in support" or "under command"?' he asked.

This was a reference to their status because there was a subtle but decisive distinction between being 'in support' where one retained the right to obey orders only given by one's own superior officer and 'under command' when one had to accept orders from the unit commander to whom one was temporary affiliated. Again this question threw me for a few seconds.

'Actually, Sir,' I said, 'I'm not sure whether they were one or the other. It was all so confused. My instinct told me that it did not matter very much because being Americans I found myself bending over backwards to brief them fully and correctly, far more than I would have done with my own chaps, so that they knew the situation and the part they were expected to play in our next moves. I found orders were not necessary because we reached mutual agreement. I suppose the logic imposed by events at the time dictated a mutually acceptable course of action.'

Alexander smiled very slightly. 'You were lucky that events did your job for you. Remember that at the end of the day no matter whom you are dealing with if you are in charge then you must give orders. Everybody has to be crystal clear about what is expected of them. There must be no doubt. Nothing less than simple confident orders will do.'

Sensing that I was somewhat abashed by this rather stern mini-lecture, he paused a second, smiled very slightly although I noticed his eyes did not soften, and added, 'However I am sure you managed very well. But remember whether they be Americans or not they are still soldiers. They expect to be given orders.'

He nodded and turned on his heel. I saluted. Suddenly things seemed to have gone somewhat icy. I felt he would be a hell of a difficult man to get to know. Perhaps I had been over familiar. Then for some unknown reason just as he reached the door I blurted out, 'Good luck, Sir.'

He paused turned half around and replied, 'Good luck to you.' He then asked me when I hoped to rejoin my regiment and I told him that it would be in a few days' time at the conclusion of my course at the school. 'We have a few rivers to cross yet,' he commented almost as an aside to the officers on the other side of the door, and as he made his exit he added a little more loudly, 'and this time the Hun will not get away.'

Then he gave me a curt dismissive but almost knowing nod, accompanied by an utterance by way of explanation which at the time I accepted as an ordinary casual remark but in the perspective of subsequent knowledge I now find most significant, it was 'because my orders will be obeyed.'

He disappeared around the corner and I was left standing somewhat numb and uncomprehending after the shock of it all, just like St Paul must have felt when God dropped in to give him a bit of advice. I saw General Alexander again that day when we all assembled to hear him give a brief talk about the forthcoming battle for the River Po. It was a brilliant incisive discourse which not only explained in very broad terms how the enemy could never get away again but how important it was to the Allied war effort in the west and the great political advantage to be gained by forestalling the Russians before they got too far into Austria. For me it was a day to remember.

When I mentioned this to General McCreery some years later and quoted to him Alexander's parting words, 'because my orders will be obeyed', McCreery said, 'I have no doubt that this was a veiled reference to Mark Clark whose behaviour on the break-out from Anzio made Alexander livid and it has rankled with him ever since. Incidentally, I do not think it was characteristic of Alexander to have had such a revealing conversation with a comparatively junior officer, if I may say so, like you, but I suspect that you established a more informal and relaxed relationship with him in a matter of minutes than many could do in years because of the spontaneous way it arose, and particularly because of your Irish connection. Alexander was a wonderful commander,' went on McCreery, 'but he could be somewhat distant and aloof at times. I think you must have pierced his reserve with that great principle of war called "surprise". You did the unexpected!'

Two of the reasons why the improbable and bizarre battles for the River Po went like clockwork clicked into place in my mind at this point. The first was that the element of surprise which General McCreery mentioned was brilliantly demonstrated in a number of ingenious ways on both tactical and strategic levels when one would have thought the Germans could never have been taken by surprise any more by anything at that late stage of the war. The second was that Alexander did in fact make damn sure that this time his intentions were carried out. Not the least reason for this was that he had two army commanders under Mark Clark called Truscott and McCreery who would have it no other way.

6. 'By Mules, Not by Men'

'Don't let on dear boy but the war will be
won by mules, not by men'
COLONEL OF GUARDS' BRIGADE AUTUMN, 1944

After the Salerno and the Cassino-Anzio setbacks the remaining period
of stalemate which lasted for nearly six months was enacted high up in
the Northern Apennines. This great massif running right across Italy
west to east with only two small coastal gaps, Pisa on the left and
Rimini on the right, had been converted by ·the Germans who had
over a year to prepare it into their most formidable defence system yet.
It was called the Gothic Line. From the autumn of 1944 to February
1945 some of the most bitter fighting in certainly the most appalling
terrain took place. It was the nadir of the Italian campaign. Yet only
a few months before the Allies in Italy had experienced heady days.

Rome had fallen. This had immediately preceded the D-Day invasion
of France itself. There was an elation born of the smell of victory, a
war of movement, and the sense of well-being engendered by a long
spell of warm sunny weather. An advance of well over one hundred
miles was made from Rome to the gates of Florence between 5th June
and the third week in July when the River Arno was reached by the
Fifth Army. The enemy was in full retreat. Many thousands of prisoners
were taken and thousands of their vehicles were destroyed or abandoned
as they ran out of petrol. But then the momentum started to slacken. In
the middle of those fateful days of such high promise, events conspired
to dash the cup of total victory from Alexander's lips. It seems incredible
but the simple fact is that this only happened because he ran out of
men. That this came about not by enemy action, nor by sickness, nor
by battle weariness nor by the expansion of the battle fronts, nor even
by any act of God, it will be consequently hard to understand. The
reason for it was that there was another battle raging at this point
in time which the Americans won and the British lost. It was a political
battle involving Roosevelt, General Marshall and General Eisenhower

75

on one side and Churchill, Alanbrooke and Alexander on the other. It resulted in the opinion of many including Mark Clark who was very much on the British side in this matter, in the most disastrous decision for the future of the free world for which so many had already laid down their lives.

The British element led by doughty Churchill wanted to capitalise on the success in Italy to move forward to the Alps, to invade Austria, and above all to move into the Balkans via Yugoslavia, for which devastating thrust both Tito and Alexander had their plans for co-operation well advanced. That all this was quite on the cards there is no doubt because the German forces in the southern Mediterranean were in disarray, harassed as they were by the Allied armies in Italy and the increasing menace of the Yugoslav and Greek partisans. This would have meant that the Russian advance into Central Europe would have been curtailed, and the political advantages which they have now enjoyed for so long and which we have so bitterly regretted would probably have been denied to them.

The Americans on the other hand wanted to open up a new front instead, at the expense of the forces in Italy by invading the south of France through Marseilles. This was codenamed Anvil and was calculated to assist the Overlord offensive, the codename for the D-Day invasion of northern France which of course had become the cynosure of the whole world.

By the end of June 1944, the opposing camps were in utter disagreement. Churchill and his British Chiefs of Staff and advisers were very reluctant to sacrifice the campaign in Italy now that it was bearing fruit and fully supported Alexander's concept of drawing away German reserves from the Western Front by using Italy as the platform for a thrust into the Balkans. Furthermore, they believed that now that Eisenhower's bridgehead for Overlord was secure there were means available for reinforcing his effort more directly than through Marseilles. The Americans were totally opposed to changing Anvil. They stated categorically their wish to put as many United States divisions into France as possible which was where they said the critical battles lay, and besides, they pointed out, the large French contingent in Italy could be far more appropriately deployed from every point of view and not forgetting the need to take General De Gaulle's aspirations into account, in liberating France.

On 28th June Churchill sent a memorandum to Roosevelt in a direct appeal to secure a decision in favour of Alexander's initiative in Italy. On 29th June, only one day later, Roosevelt replied that he could not

agree to Americans being 'diverted' to the Balkans and Anvil should
stand. He then added something which prompted Churchill to make
one of his most significant and prophetic pronouncements. Roosevelt
suggested that if they could not agree the matter must be referred to
Stalin. It seems incredible now that in a matter of such far reaching
military and especially political consequences for the Western World
Roosevelt should be so naive as to wish to refer it to arbitration by, of
all people, Stalin! It was almost as if a demarcation dispute between
managements of two companies was being referred to the secretary of
the trade union with the biggest interest in their employees. The
ultimate beneficiary of the judgement was bound to be the arbitrator
himself.

Within forty-eight hours Churchill sent his last appeal to Roosevelt
which made this consideration crystal clear. Having reminded Roosevelt
that it was he himself who at an earlier conference at Teheran had
first proposed operations based on the northern Italy/Adriatic Sector,
he went on:

> I have considered your suggestion that we should lay our respective
> cases before Stalin . . . I do not know what he would say if the issue
> was put to him to decide. On military grounds he might be greatly
> interested in the eastward movement of Alexander's Army which . . .
> might produce the most far-reaching results. *On a long term political
> view, he might prefer that the British and Americans should do their
> share in France in this very hard fighting that is to come and that
> East, Middle and Southern Europe, should fall naturally into his
> control.* It is better to settle the matter for ourselves and between
> ourselves.

Churchill then indicated that if the decision for Anvil was still pressed
this could only be accepted by the British Government under a
'solemn protest' but he added, 'I need scarcely say that we shall do
our best to make a success of anything that is undertaken.'

In the event the Americans prevailed.

It is utterly ironic therefore to record that at the very moment when
the Allies were withdrawing seven of their best divisions from Italy, the
Germans were moving no less than eight divisions plus additional
supporting troops over and above that already impressive reinforcement
to bolster their defence of Italy. The strong became weaker, and the
weak became stronger. It was inevitable that a stalemate should follow,
but not before Alexander's Fifteenth Army Group had effected with

their depleted and battle weary forces an heroic breakthrough of the German Gothic Line. This, given a little more luck and a couple of the divisions of which he had been deprived, might have enabled Alexander to deal the enemy a mortal blow in the Po Valley before the dreadful Italian winter set in.

The Fifth Army which had lost three United States divisions and four French divisions for what Alexander described as the 'strategically useless attack on the south of France' stormed the Futa Pass, the highest key-point in the Gothic Line from which could be seen over the miles and miles of subsidiary peaks beyond the distant and gleaming prospect of the Po Valley itself. By the end of September 1944, the Eighth Army had turned the right flank of the Gothic Line at Rimini and had edged forward threatening to outflank the gigantic mountain ranges which separated the Fifth Army from its objectives.

To have got so far when the German resistance was now as rugged as the formidable natural obstacles the Allies faced was a great achievement. But the price was grievous. The Eighth Army alone in its last few weeks of operations suffered over fourteen thousand casualties, more than they had lost at El Alamein, and over two hundred of their precious tanks were destroyed. Worse still when they had broken away at last from the stranglehold of the Apennines and were anticipating the comparative luxury of a free range war in the plains beyond, they found in fact not only more damnable and bloody rivers to cross, but a treacherous terrain of dykes, ditches, swamps, and deceptive hills and undulations which afforded the tenacious and skilful enemy his best protective cover yet.

So it was that in mid-October when the rains came, and when the key points in the Po Valley of Bologna and Ravenna were little more than a day's march from the Fifth and Eighth Armies respectively, Alexander decided reluctantly to abandon any hope of destroying the German armies in Italy until the spring of 1945. The fact that he was still contemplating ultimate success can only be regarded as a blind act of faith and almost foolhardy optimism. Towards the end of 1944 he had nothing going for him. His armies had been depleted to the tune of ten divisions or more, allowing for those snatched from him for the invasion of southern France and the casualties from sickness and enemy action. Those that were left were battle weary to the point of near-exhaustion. Physical obstacles of a magnitude never previously encountered in the shape of the highest and most rugged part of the Apennines barred their way. Torrential rainstorms turned the entire front into a mud bath in which roads collapsed, vehicles could not move, even the most powerful tanks could not manoeuvre without shedding their tracks, and swollen streams and rivers far from cleansing their erratic tracts dispensed instead a tenacious glue of silt and sluggish slime. There was a shortage of food, ammunition, and even such creature comforts as socks. Everything in fact was in short supply. In some areas the guns and mortars were rationed to ten rounds a day, just enough to make sure they could still fire. The worst thing about a soldier's war is not the prospect of dying or losing a leg or an arm, it is the sheer hell of discomfort. Agonising, shivering, sodden, misery not just for an hour or so but for day after day after day. Here everything conspired to produce the ultimate in such misery.

There was not even the crumb of comfort that the enemy might be suffering equally. On the contrary they had been re-inforced; the frequency of their harassing fire from their big '108' guns and their latest multi-barrelled mortars made it clear that not for them was rationing any necessity; and above all they enjoyed comfort of billets they had reconnoitred and occupied months previously.

Never was morale so low and not the least pang of despair was the realisation that we who had fought for so long with the Eighth Army in its victorious march of many thousands of miles from Alamein to the Northern Apennines were now discarded. Italy had been reduced to a secondary campaign. One in which it was hoped that a few expendable troops could manage to keep a few Germans occupied while the fickle gaze of the world shifted to the great theatres of war elsewhere. Something of the bitterness and indomitable humour of the British Soldier was reflected in the slogan chalked on the vehicles carrying him forward to do battle yet again which said 'we are the D-Day dodgers'. The ironic acknowledgement of the glory and publicity accorded those making the invasion of France said it all.

Perhaps the only thing which kept the thread of sanity from snapping in many of us during these miserable months was the humour of a cartoon in what purported to be our army newspaper and which was read avidly whenever served up erratically with the rations. It was called the 'Two Types' and was drawn by Jon, the famous cartoonist of the *Daily Mail*, depicted two officers with outrageous moustaches who persisted in wearing the equally outrageous and eccentric dress they adopted in their desert campaigns. In fact they were so addicted to their desert experience that they were never seen without their fly whisks. Somehow or other the nostalgia they provoked with their echo of greater days hit exactly the right note at a time when there was nothing else to laugh about. I recall one cartoon in which our 'Two Types' were holding mugs of tea while standing in the mud in the familiar rain-soaked Italian landscape. One was leaning forward with what looked like a large sugar castor in his hand and asking solicitously of the other, 'Have a little sand in your tea, old man?'

To understand the trials and tribulations of the Allied armies during this ghastly and frustrating period there is no substitute for describing the routine dangers and drudgery faced by small sections of men, and who faced them not for a week or two but month after month after month. The support group of heavy mortars and medium machine gun companies which I commanded were in the line without relief from October 1944 for one hundred and twenty-three consecutive days. This was in a large and thinly manned sector thousands of feet up in the highest part of the Apennines in which the 78th British Division was the link between the Americans of the Fifth Army on their left and the British Eighth Army on their right. It would have been impossible to have fought and survived in this God-forsaken hell without two things. The one was the combined courage and humour of that improbable hero – Tommy Atkins. The other was that extraordinary and much maligned four-legged hero, the mule. There have been many famous components of the modern army to which the word corps is applied and usually with the prefix 'Royal' to give them rightly merited status like Royal Tank Corps, Royal Medical Corps, and Royal Army Service Corps. But in Italy it is true to say that in the mountainous country over which almost the entire campaign was fought we would have got nowhere without the formation of a corps which normally would have been beneath the dignity of any self-respecting staff officer to suggest. This was the Mule Corps. In terms of manpower and animals it represented the equivalent of more than three divisions. It had over 30,000 mules alone. Some were drawn from Italy itself and reinforced with importations from Palestine, Sicily, Cyprus, but the largest consignments came from countries as far away as Argentine and Brazil.

To illustrate the point I will quote verbatim the report first of all of Sergeant J. Tuvey of my regiment. His description of what a small mule supply train had to endure in a typical journey by night needs no embellishment. The names of the locations he mentions are not important. They were simply names on a map which were like any of the hundreds of others to be found in the highest altitudes of those forlorn Apennine ranges.

'We gathered at the mule point at Appolinare in the afternoon.

Captain C. E. Cullen was in charge of our train, which consisted of forty mules, twenty Italian muleteers, five British soldiers, and myself. We loaded the animals with mortar bombs, machine gun ammunition, rations, wireless spare parts, etc., and, most important of all, *rum*! There was another mule train also waiting near by, which was to leave before ours. In addition there were several other mule trains at Sassaleone which were to use the track to Ripiano as well, so timing was of the utmost importance.

'We started about 1605 hours. Great, heavy clouds hung overhead, and any minute we expected our daily downpour. Far in front we could see the other mule trains crawling like ants over the mountains. The going was very hard in the mud, but we were making fairly good progress, and I had high hopes of eating in Ronchi by 1930 hours. No one spoke, and the only sounds were the jangling of harness and the squelching of mud. Then suddenly, things began to happen. It was just about dark and the rain was starting, when there was a short whistle and a "crump", then another, then another, and we realised that the first mule train was being well and truly "stonked". Captain Cullen immediately halted the column and we took the opportunity to adjust our gas-capes as the rain was sweeping down in great gusts. The shelling didn't last long and in a few minutes we had started, bending forward against the rain.

'Immediately we began to descend into Ripiano valley, I realised that nothing we had gone through so far was going to compare with what was to come. The mud got thicker and deeper, until in parts it reached up to my thigh. As darkness was now well and truly upon us, black as ink, I couldn't see farther than the mule in front of me. First one mule, then two, get stuck in the mire, and in their frantic efforts to free themselves they threw their loads. One man who got waist-deep in the ooze was pulled out minus his boots, socks, and gaiters. I, at the rear had only a vague idea what was going on from the shouts and yells. I had previously fallen over the dead bodies of both Germans and Americans at the top of the ridge; what with those and the driving rain now worse than ever, coupled with the terrific job of getting one foot in front of the other.

'I realised that the Italian muleteers wouldn't stand very much more and would be deserting at any moment. I decided to go forward and give Captain Cullen a hand. By great luck I soon stumbled into him and he told me that he was going to try to find an alternative route. Many of the mules were now belly deep in the mud, and in the pitch darkness and rain it was impossible to know how many we had lost.

'As I was floundering around trying to reorganise our column, I was suddenly confronted by a mule train coming the other way. In vain I tried to stop it running into ours. They just merged, and to add to the confusion the original train, which had set out before us, had now collected its scattered forces and was even now up to the rear of our lot. So there were about a hundred mules and men, feet deep in mud, in a horrid tangled mess on a pitch-black night in driving rain. To this was added the fear of further shelling. It was just then, when things looked really grim, that I had my second stroke of luck. I stumbled into Captain Cullen once more, who told me that he had found a new way down the hill to the stream in the valley.

'Mules were lying everywhere, their kicking had shot the loads off all over the place, and one mule, I remember, had fallen into a disused slit-trench with only its saddle supporting it on either side of the hole. We started to sort all this mess out, first collecting our own men and leading them on to firmer ground, and then by grabbing any Italian we saw and forcing him to follow. Finally, after what seemed an age we got under way again, and I still had the *rum*!

'On reaching the river at the bottom of the hill, we again ran into further trouble. The rope across was still there, but the first step that Captain Cullen took into it covered his thighs. We managed to pull him out and I suggested a good swig of rum. This did the trick, for he made the other side first time. Then after endless trouble we got everyone else across and got to Ripiano without further incident.

'There, we started to sort out the mules with the machine gun kit and those with the mortar kit, as Captain Cullen had still to go down the valley to Ronchi with the latter. You can therefore imagine our astonishment when we found that we had six mules over and above our original number! The Italian muleteers had simply decided to follow the main party wherever it was going.'

This was the sort of occurrence which prompted an officer of the Grenadier Guards to remark to me as a nonchalant aside when we were both supervising the departure of mule trains from our Tactical HQ near Appolinare, 'Don't let on, dear boy, but the war will be won by mules, not by men.'

While all this was going on by night it has to be remembered that other things were going on as well both by night and by day which did nothing to help. Mini battles were being fought. Patrols were going out and sometimes coming back. Men were fighting to save their equipment if not their lives. Men were dying of sickness and of fatigue. Carnage, chaos and mayhem were no longer words. They were reality. One comes face to face with it in the following report given by Major Byrne Foxwell, a brother officer of mine, in our regimental history *The Kensingtons.*

Once again forget the place names and technical terms. Just let the narrative stir the imagination and envisage the dreariness, dramas, and melancholy which linked the hours and days of all those men who, as Churchill said, 'fought in one line victoriously'. Also mark the humour and humanity of Byrne Foxwell, the clues to the kind of understanding and leadership he possessed and which inspired his men to hold the line.

'On 19th October, 36 Brigade captured Monte La Pieve which was the cue for the Irish Brigade to attack Monte Spaduro. Accordingly the 1st Battalian Royal Irish Fusiliers took up positions for their assault on Spaduro that night.

'The Brigade was particularly keen to have our mortars in support. This was real mortar country : the bombs in their vertical descent could get right into the enemy's gullies : the gunners couldn't do the same thing because of the crest-clearance problem.

'Lieutenant Dick Gray found a mortar position, a deep gully just behind Gesso. His platoon occupied their new positions by 20.00 hours, about half an hour before the attack was to go in. Meanwhile Dick Gray and his Observation Post party, consisting of Corporal Dennis, a wireless operator, two mules and two wireless sets, went off to join the Royal Irish Fusiliers at Point 416. They had a nasty trip beyond Monte La Pieve, groping their way along a white tape through a mine-field and being 'stonked' all the way. They eventually arrived intact. No 4 Platoon gave supporting fire in the attack which the Faughs (Royal Irish Fusiliers) pressed forward with great gallantry. They reported the capture of Spaduro at 05.15 hours on 20th October. At 06.00 hours the enemy counter-attacked in strength. The two leading companies of the Faughs fought stubbornly and heroically but against superier odds and they fought to the end until they ran out of ammunition. Spaduro was yet to be won. The Brigadier ordered the 2nd Battalian London Irish to take it on the night of the 20th. For this purpose our other mortar platoon was required. No 3 platoon took up a position near No 4 platoon. Dick Gray now came under the orders of the London Irish and controlled the fire of both platoons.

'No 12 platoon machine guns joined the London Irish for the attack. On the way, the platoon's wireless set was deposited in a minefield by the mule which was supposed to be carrying it. With somewhat foolhardy gallantry Sergeant Waters retrieved it (much to the annoyance, no doubt, of the operator, who thought the mule had given him a temporary relief from his labours).

'After the previous night's battle, Jerry's gunners had turned the heat right on. No 4 platoon had three mortar bombs on their mortar position. Luckily nobody was hurt. The chaps dug deeper into their holes and hoped for the best.

'The London Irish attack went in at midnight 20th/21st October with the limited objective of Little Spaduro – Hill 387.

'As in Faughs' attack, the enemy at Spinello House caused trouble. The London Irish by-passed this strongpoint and pressed on towards their objective. There they were pinned to the ground by the Spinello garrison and by the enemy on Hill 387 itself. All day on 21st October they remained unable to move. At dusk they continued the attack, but they were withdrawn by their CO six hours later without dislodging the Hun from Hill 387.'

This attack on Hill 387 which Byrne Foxwell describes became almost a family affair because apart from his own mortar platoons which were in action all day of 21st October, it so happened that my mortars and machine guns were also able to fire in support, and the combined hate on both sides continued for a further forty-eight hours non-stop. But still that stubborn hill could not be taken.

So a new plan to capture it and the higher ground behind it called Spaduro was made. This was now to involve four battalions, two from 11 Brigade and two from the Irish Brigade. The latter were told to take on Hill 387 again. Byrne Foxewell continues:

'The assault by the Skins (the 2nd Battalion Royal Inniskilling Fusiliers) was timed for 22.30 hours, but a lengthy approach march down a river-bed with mules necessitated starting out at 16.30 hours. In order to cover up their noise, the London Irish were ordered to start cleaning up Spinello at the same time. This was a bit tough, as it meant a direct daylight assault on the garrison which had been the cause of upsetting two battalion attacks already.

'Lieutenant-Colonel Bredin of the London Irish sent a patrol out to Casa Spinello with the objective of bringing back a prisoner who might give information of the enemy's lay-out there and on Hill 387. Upon the success of this patrol depended everything, from their own lives to the success or failure of four-battalion attack that night.

'It was certain that once the Hun noticed them the patrol would be extremely lucky to make the return journey of 400 yards to our FDL's (Forward Defended Localities). Among other precautions, Lieutenant-Colonel Bredin told No 12 Platoon that he wanted a machine gun section jacked up and ready to take on Spinello as soon as they opened fire. Whether Sergeant W. Taylor was given the job or whether he prevented anyone else from doing it, history doesn't relate; in any case it was right up his street. He decided not to use his normal direct-fire positions in case they should be made the target for Teuton gunnery forever after. He found another position where, with Corporal Henshall as his No 2, he mounted his machine gun, watched like a hawk and waited.

'The patrol crawled stealthily forward and reached Spinello un-noticed. They pounced on a slit-trench; shot two Huns, and collared the third. The surprised garrison opened up with all they had got – so did Sergeant Taylor. A personal duel ensued between Sergeant Taylor and two Spandaus in the house. Sergeant Taylor silenced one Spandau and kept the attention of the other until at last the patrol came back with its prisoner.

'The Hun talked. His information was invaluable. It included the defences of Spinello and the general set-up of the enemy on Hill 387. The information came just in time for the London Irish main attack which started at 16.30 hours. It was accompanied by a weighty artillery fire programme and innumerable juicy "crumps" from our two mortar platoons directed by Dick Gray. Once again Sergeant Taylor took on his Spandau.

'The London Irish got Spinello, at a price, and were able to hold it against three counter-attacks. This accomplished, the other three battalions were able to start their assaults at 22.30 hours. The attacks were costly but all were successful, and all our immediate objectives were won. Lieutenant-Colonel Bredin expressed his great appreciation of the work done by both the mortars and the machine-guns during the three days 21st–23rd October. Sergeant Taylor received an immediate award of the Military Medal.'

One of the irritating aspects of newly won positions was that they were invariably followed by the re-deployment of the units which had sup-ported the attack. This meant that no sooner had one got dug in and achieved some comfort in a static role than one had to dig oneself out and start all over again. One of Byrne Foxwell's machine gun platoons moving just a short distance had to use twenty-two mules to shift their kit. The mules floundered and slithered on the slimy mountainside to such an extent that it became a 24 hour operation. Much of the time was simply spent chasing up half a dozen mule-loads of equipment that had been shed on the way. A further account of the appalling conditions encountered is given by Byrne Foxwell :

'On 25th October No 3 Platoon (mortars) were ordered to move round to Ripiano on the left flank to give defensive fire to the Skins. They had to borrow twenty men from the Faughs to help dig up their base-plates and move their kit on to the road. Six RASC jeeps and trailers started to ferry them off to Ripiano, where they shared a house with a mortar platoon of another Group. The platoon's move coincided with the beginning of torrential rain, which continued without a stop for forty-eight hours. The route to Ripiano crossed the River Sillaro at the San Clemente ford. When the first convoy crossed, the water was a foot deep. Two hours later when the second convoy came to cross, the river was a raging torrent and the ford three feet deep. It was by then pitch dark. As all Kensingtons knew, the ford was a favourite 'stonking' ground for the Jerry gunners. Sergeant Walder made a game attempt to take the first jeep over, but as soon as it went into the water it was swept down the river with trailer, bombs and all the rest. Sergeant Walder and the driver managed to scramble out of the water. This half of No 3 Platoon was stranded at San Clemente in the haunted houses for the next three days.

'Lieutenant Dick Gray, Corporal Dennis and their OP party were relieved on the 25th, having been at Pt 416 – the HQ first of the Faughs and then of the London Irish – since the 19th. They had had very little sleep during those six days. The enemy's shell-fire had been so incessant that they hardly dared to go outside to relieve nature. Communication with the mortar position had been a constant problem. They were lucky if the telephone cable lasted half an hour before being cut by shell-fire. Their No 22 Wireless Set had been put out of action during a 'stonk', but they managed to scrape along with their No 18 Set when the telephone went dead.

'Their relief was Lieutenant Harvey Shillidy and his OP party. They went to the HQ of the Royal Inniskilling Fusiliers. Just as they were about to set off, one of their two mules collapsed and died, without having the decency to give a warning murmur of complaint. Mules were like that. This incident merely serves as a typical illustration of the sort of frustrating things which were continually happening to everybody.

'It was on this rainy day that No 12 platoon were ordered back to Appolinare for two days' rest. They arrived at dusk – all soaked to the skin and thoroughly worn out after six days and nights under heavy fire. Two of them were sick, but they could not be evacuated as the Division's maintenance road to the rear had fallen away in a landslide: Appolinare, a tiny village of about ten houses, was already choked with 36 Brigade HQ and the Irish Brigade HQ. Half the platoon were squeezed into a stable already filled with other soliders. An inch of water stood on the floor. There was no question of dry clothes. The best that could be done was to light fires inside the stable; huddle closely together; and hopefully hang socks over the fire on sticks.'

It so happens I had a little outhouse about 12 feet square as my Group HQ and with fellow feeling for those gallant and exhausted men of my regiment I managed to find room for fifteen of them to sleep on my mud floor – beautifully dry mud. They slept on it with grateful hearts, oozing water like sponges.

Sergeant 'Tiny' Waters was the commander of these men and, believe it or not, he had no trousers; they had been washed off the mountain in the deluge. Prompted by a desire to maintain Regimental prestige, Byrne Foxwell had lent 'Tiny' his denim trousers (and he never got them back). His account continues:

'The 26th October dawned. Icy rain was still pouring down. It had now been raining continuously for twenty hours. At 10.00 hours Sergeant Shoobert – acting mortar position officer of No 4 Platoon – reported that their once dry gulley was now a raging torrent; one of the mortar baseplates was under water; the slit-trenches had filled in; the men's kit was swamped; and soil was falling down the side of the gulley. At 11.00 hours Sergeant Shoobert reported that one of the mortars had only one inch of muzzle showing above the water; the torrent had risen three feet; the whole mortar position was being swamped by water and landslides; he had only one mortar above the water-level. He was ordered to keep his one mortar in action and to salvage the other mortar sights and any other equipment he could. At 12.00 hours wireless and telephone communication with the platoon ceased altogether.

'An hour later, Corporal Gladding reported to Group HQ that one of the mortars had been completely buried in a landslide and that the last remaining mortar had to be dismantled to save it from a similar fate. When he left the platoon the men were working as hard as possible to salvage what kit they could. He said it was all he could physically do to get himself out of the gulley.

'Captain Depinna – commanding the mortar company – went off to help salvage his platoon. By diligent searching he found an isolated house about half a mile away. He managed by degrees to get the platoon into it that day. Every man was completely exhausted and numbed with cold and wet. If they had not found that house, the whole lot would have been hospital cases. For instance, Corporal Sewell was dazed for days afterwards from his magnificent feat in maintaining vital signal communications for five days and nights without relief.

'On the 27th, No 11 platoon, clinging to Hill 387, were even worse off. There was no shelter whatever; if they tried to dig a slit-trench it immediately filled with water; there was nowhere to sit except on the muddy slope at an angle of 45 degrees. Ten of their number collapsed with exposure or trench foot and had to be evacuated as sick. Corporal Simmance invented a system whereby two men, crouched under their gas-capes, lit a small No 3 petrol cooker, brewed up some tea, and tried to keep warm at the same time. The only snag was that there was only one cooker per ten men and a great scarcity of petrol. The man who preserved the rest of the platoon from hospital that day was the self-appointed cook – Private Adshead – who, by some miracle, brewed up a dixie of tea.

'The only platoon to relieve them was No 12 Platoon which was "resting" in Appolinare. They were completely unfit. All were suffering from trench foot in some degree; in thirty-six hours at Appolinare they had not even got dry. All that could be said was that they had had a decent square meal cooked by the Group HQ cook, 'Topper' Brown. The whole thing was fantastic; but for the fact that the rifle battalions had suffered great casualties and, like us, large numbers were sick, we would have said with excellent reason, that the thing was "not on". So that night, with boots as heavy as lead, No 12 Platoon went up to relieve No 11 Platoon with the Skins on Hill 387. Just before the relief, Sergeant Ganley's section carried out a harassing fire shoot at the Skins' request.

'The only place for No 11 Platoon to go was a dirty, poky, partly demolished house in view of the enemy just in front of Gesso; they thought themselves very lucky to get it. It was only half a mile from their gun positions but they were so exhausted, their feet were so sore, and the mud was so appalling that it took some of them four hours to walk it. When taking stock of the platoon the next day it was found that fifteen men had trench foot or 'flu; but from then on they began to dry out gradually.

'First No 12 platoon on the 25th, then No 4 platoon on the 26th, and now No 11 platoon on the 27th were all exhausted to the limit of endurance. They all knew that no relief was possible and that they stick it out somehow. The whole thing was a nightmare.'

One of the stupid things which contributed to the nightmare described by Byrne Foxwell was the great sock scandal. All the platoons wanted socks; the whole Army wanted socks; but we were told that there were none in Italy or even in England. We didn't get the socks. Shortly afterwards, this scandal was reported to a visiting MP. He cabled the Prime Minister and quite a lot of socks turned up rather smartly.

The nightmare was not confined to the platoons. Captain Alf Oakes (Foxwell's Second-in-Command) had one every minute. Every hour of every day he was bombarded with demands from the platoons : to send up a petrol cooker here; a machine gun tripod there; insatiable demands for socks, foot powder, gas-capes, great coats, battledress, clean clothes of all kinds, to say nothing of rum, rations, and ammunition. Every bit of it had to be loaded on a mule. Byrne Foxwell paid his special tribute :

'There was no more noble work done in the Group than by the driver mechanics (now muleteers) who piloted the mule trains which were supplied by an Italian mule company. Night after night, through the Spaduro battles and the rains that followed, they groped their way along, climbing the steep, muddy ascent out of Appolinare – avoiding the swamp where a dozen mules had sunk by Gesso cemetery – passing the bogged-down tanks on the way to Gesso – picking their way through the mine-field – quickening the pace through the ruins of Gesso to avoid the almost inevitable "stonking" – floundering along the nightmare track of interminable length to Hill 387 – arriving after a four-hour journey at Sergeant Ganley's section at the very end of the world, only to find that some vital sandbag had dropped off a mule. Then the same procedure going back – getting very hungry – perspiring with the effort of squelching along in the mud – flopping into it to avoid a shell screaming down – stumbling into a shell-hole that wasn't there on the way up. At last, back in Appolinare, the muleteer got his well-earned one-twentieth bottle of rum and fell into some straw to sleep.

'It was lucky for us that the man in charge of mule trains from

Appolinare forward was Sergeant John Bowley. There was no more efficient and energetic soldier in my Group – qualities which were entirely eclipsed by the fact that he was our Secret Weapon against despair – our private Tommy Handley. We loved his non-stop comment which made for us, and us alone, such ordinary things as a cigar-smoking GI, an unshaven Italian gentleman, or a dusky Indian muleteer, objects of ribald mirth.'

Following the period Byrne Foxwell has described there were no further offensive operations. They were impossible because the whole front was one colossal morass, and battle casualties and sickness had taken a huge toll. All the Fifth and Eighth Army efforts were needed to keep the forward troops supplied with the barest essentials. During the weeks that followed the only possible activity was provided by the Royal Artillery and our machine guns and heavy mortar units who worked night and day on harassing fire tasks. These were very sporadic being strictly limited by the amount of ammunition that could be brought forward. Even so the dramas of the day to day battle for survival went on as Byrne Foxwell's report so vividly illustrates.

'On 18th November the Irish Brigade side-stepped to the left to take over a brigade sector from 5 Division. The area was in the hills below Monte Grande to the left of San Clemente. In some respects it was not so bad as the place we had left. The platoon areas were much less muddy. Admin problems were easier because rations could be taken up in daylight, except to No 12 platoon at Casa Luca. The Casa Luca position was an evil and isolated spot from the beginning. The day that No 12 platoon occupied it, they were heavily mortared. Private Ward was wounded. One bomb burst in the cooking department – Private Adshead narrowly missed being sent for a six. The place was always being "stonked". The platoon just had to live underground in a state of tension. One night Leading Sergeant Ridgeway left his tin hat outside his dug-out; next morning it was riddled like a colander.

'Bitterest loss of all was on 2nd December. Lieutenant Harvey Shillidy and Corporal Lee were killed there by a mortar bomb just as they were leaving their OP at dusk. Harvey hadn't missed a battle since the campaign started. He, like Dick Gray, was so famed in the Irish Brigade for his reliability and mastery of the 4.2″ mortar, that no Irish Battalion ever went into action without demanding either "Harvey" or "Dick". Expressions of grief at his loss came from all battalions, but to us his loss was more personal. Harvey was a brother in our family and we loved him for his charming qualities no less than we admired him for his gallant conduct in battle over a very long period. Corporal Lee was one of those quiet, efficient chaps who was also extremely popular, and we felt his loss very keenly indeed.

'No 12 Platoon occupied this position for two months without relief. It was one of the nastiest places imaginable. Owing to the shortage of officers it was commanded during most of this period by NCOs, notably CQMS McGowan and Sergeant Ganley, backed up by such seasoned and indomitable warriors as Corporal Simmance, Corporal Thomas, and Leading Sergeant Ridgeway. Ridgeway took command of the platoon for a short spell; instead, he was thought to have been in hospital: his tummy couldn't digest anything at all, but he flatly refused to report sick.

'No 11 Platoon – now commanded by Lieutenant John Young – occupied a position near the Battalion HQ in that area. It was not nearly so bad as the Casa Luca position, but it had its full share of trouble. The place was like a rabbit warren; everyone lived in huge slit-trenches which, being sandy, kept reasonably dry and clean.

'If John Young wasn't swanning on the sky-line with some wild Irishman – teasing the Germans – he was stirring up his platoon or roundly castigating some poor, innocent soldier, or being severely ticked off himself by his own batman. Alternatively, he would sit in his slit-trench listening to the BBC on his No 18 set – sipping from some secret hoard of vino and drafting some vitriolic signal to Group HQ demanding to know why his platoon never got enough food or indeed any food at all. John was a constant source of entertainment to his platoon and the Irish Brigade as well. Brigadier Scott wrote in his diary: "There was John Young – a great enthusiast who fired his weapons on any and every possible occasion and provocation."

'Quoting further from the Brigadier's diary, it is recorded that on the evening of 26th November, No 11 machine-gun Platoon did a very good shoot on Cereto which obviously had results, as Sergeant Callinan (infantry listening-patrol commander) heard screams afterwards. On that day also a mortar "stonk" (from our mortars) on Tamagnin coincided with the entry of a Hun ration party, so it was probable there was a bag. There were certainly some results that day, as at dawn the next day German stretcher-bearers and an ambulance were seen busy at their Advance Dressing Station.'

But the Germans were very good at 'stonking' too. It was far from being one-sided. Along the entire front they delivered massive salvoes of shells and mortar bombs at unpredictable intervals. For typical examples I can do no better than quote again from Foxwell's personal diary. He says :

'*Tuesday, Dec 5th* : Considerable enemy harassing fire with heavy mortars in forward area. Both sections of 11 platoon received "stonks". Corporal Henshall was badly wounded in the chest. Private Hogg and Lance Corporal Edwards were wounded at the same time. Private Lee of the other section was also wounded. Private Shackall was deafened by blast but he remained at duty.

'*Wednesday, Dec 6th* : Very foggy in the morning in the Forward Defended Localities. More than one enemy patrol entered under cover of fog at 07.17 hours. Skins had one man taken prisoner from OP about 75 yards from the nearest 12 platoon position. Both machine-gun platoons had 100% stand-to all day. No 3 platoon (mortars) fired DF (Defensive Fire) at call of Faughs. Slight harassing fire on 11 and 12 positions during the night.

'*Thursday, Dec 7th* : 11 and 12 platoons harassed by enemy mortars all day. Enemy harassing fire continued during the night. No 1 Gun, No 1 section, 11 platoon, was hit by mortar shrapnel. The barrel casing was punctured beyond repair.

'So it went on with the machine-gun platoons day after day. Little wonder that tempers got frayed and nerves became screwed up to bursting-point. For instance, there was the occasion when Sergeant Ganley was furious with rage when his sentry at Casa Luca fired his machine-gun at three Germans 200 yards away and killed only one of them.

'While No 3 Platoon were at Ripiano, the mortar line stood 100 yards in front of their house. The intervening ground was usually 1 foot under water, as the River Sillaro was always flooding. When there was a call for Defensive Fire the platoon, with the mighty Corporal Searle in the lead, would go roaring away to the mortars attired in martial dress, less trousers plus shoes, canvas, pairs, 1. They left their boots and trousers high and dry in the house. When No 3 Platoon's house at Ripiano was hit on 22nd November, Sergeant Bryan organised the salvage of nearly all the platoon equipment. In the face of exploding tank ammunition, it was a very fine achievement. Luckily, the only casualty was Private J. Jones, who got some shrapnel in his leg. After that, the platoon had to live in muddy dug-outs on the mortar line.

'They later moved to the valley behind the San Clemente valley, where they built mud and bomb-case igloos to live in. Soon after, there was a big snowstorm followed by a thaw, with the result that (a) the igloos collapsed, and (b) the language was something awful. The platoon then moved to the San Clemente valley and they were careful to build their houses on rock this time.

'In the San Clemente sector No 4 platoon had a position in the valley just above the mule point. It was a dirty, muddy place. Any digging just filled up with water, so it was a case of building up sort of igloos out of empty bomb cases and mud to keep the wind out.

'No 4 platoon's mud igloo position got rather unhealthy on account of harassing fire, so they moved further down the valley. They were given the parts of a Nissen hut and told to build it. They did.'

The ability of these soldiers to improvise anything out of anything was staggering. For example, when the official petrol burning cooker was not available they simply punched a few holes in a jerrican, warmed the petrol inside until it started to vaporise, and then put a match to it. Out shot a long flame at ground level. They bridged the flame with improvised grills on which rested improvised pots and kettles and mugs to produce hot food and beverages. Wherever there was necessity there was plenty of invention.

Each man acquired a private stock of little things which helped to make life more comfortable. For example, he would make a wire cradle for a mug out of an empty tin so that hot tea did not burn his fingers. He would acquire a pair of pliers because there was always wire to be cut or a tin to be opened. He would hoard some of the larger field dressings, not in case he was wounded, but because put together they became a handy head rest. He would appropriate a discarded German helmet, not as a souvenir, but because with the lining taken out it became a portable wash basin.

At the end of his report Byrne Foxwell summed it all up by saying :

'In conclusion, it may fairly be said that my soldiers in enduring the torments of hell day by day and in the lonely watches of the night from October to December 1944, had grown to the full stature of manhood.

'Nobody said as much, but each man felt in his bones that England had summoned him to Her service and each knew that there was only one course open : that was to stick it out.

'There was among them a code of discipline not to be found in King's Regulations. Each man had to give all he had got; there was no truck with passengers. In return he enjoyed the sublime blessing of the absolute loyalty of his fellow men – without which he would have been blown away like a leaf in the wind, if he didn't go mad first.

'If he had fought his last battle in this seemingly endless struggle, each man was entitled to feel that he had been put to the highest test and had passed with honours. If he ever went home again he could confidently look his neighbour in the eye – not arrogantly, but tempered with the knowledge that this was not only a soldiers' war; news from home, however reassuring, could not conceal the fact that it was everybody's war.'

7. 'Shifting father's grave'

'They are shifting father's grave
to build a sewer' . . .

SOLDIER OF THE BUFFS WINTER, 1944

In all these vicissitudes one wonders how the individual fulfilled his normal needs deprived as he was for months on end of anything resembling modern conveniences. How did he sleep? The glib answer is 'not very well, thank you' but in fact he learnt to cat-nap and to turn the luxury of even two hours' oblivion in wet clothes and encased like a lifeless mummy in a sodden grey blanket into the equivalent of eight hours' healthy repose. He could sleep suspended in any degree of elevation from the horizontal and diagonal to the absolute vertical when sometimes he was only supported by the stiffening of his uniform as the mud dried out.

In less adverse conditions he slept in a small portable and very personal little bedroom called a 'bivvy' (bivouac). This olive green or brown canvas abode about 6′ by 3′ often had a mosquito net lining and could be quickly erected by attaching the roof cords to trees and then pulling out the sides and pegging them down. The digging of a slit trench or tiny dug-out underneath the roof added an unbelievable dimension of comfort and cosiness and above all for safety. In fact if one was up front the first thing one did, and I mean the first thing (taking precedence even over the urgency of attending to the forces of nature, a euphemism constantly used by a journalist I once knew to explain his rush to the lavatory) was to dig in. The carving out of a shallow trench in the earth or rock to enable one to crouch below ground level meant the difference between being killed by enemy fire or staying alive. It was as simple as that. Only very rarely indeed did a slit trench, once described by Bob Hope as a GI's outsize boot without laces, get a direct hit. Therefore, an essential piece of equipment carried carefully into action by Tommy Atkins was a small stout shovel with a tiny handle and listed in the army indenting form as 'Tool, entrenching, Mark I'.

How did he eat? Once again the glib answer is 'only spasmodically'. In fact the army was superb in supplying the ingredients and right down to section level one of the miracles of human versatility was demonstrated always by the emergence of somebody who could cook a passable meal. The basic rations required to keep a man not only alive but fighting fit were referred to by the soldiers simply as 'compo'. This was in abbreviation of 'composite' meaning a blend of rations packed in a rectangular wooden box. This was easy to stack inside a small truck or on any willing mule. It contained enough food for three meals for fourteen men for one day, and conversely so well balanced that it could feed one man three meals a day for fourteen days. How is that for ingenuity! Furthermore, there were three or four kinds of 'compo' boxes having a variation of contents so that the diet did not become too monotonous. They all had tea, chocolate, biscuits, sweet tinned milk and tinned rashers of bacon in common but the tinned meats and puddings varied. The latter included an absolutely delicious creamed rice and creamy sultana roll for which I used to trade my bully beef, or even my precious cigarettes.

Creature comforts such as cigarettes, whisky, gin, rum, and even confectionery were ferried forward with reverence right up to the front line, so that every soldier at some suitable moment could get a swig of something. But these moments were often long delayed and the rations were always in short supply. The general practice was to hoard the bottles at platoon and company level and then as soon as the men came out of the line for a two or three day break to have a monumental piss-up. These were the occasions when impromptu concert parties and madcap antics when anybody could do anything a little bizarre like taking their vest off without removing their jacket or falling off a chair backwards provoked uncontrollable hysteria.

Once I witnessed the amazing spectacle of five of my irrepressible cockneys doing a 'knees-up' dance without once moving their legs. The fact was that in their alcoholic euphoria they had remembered to do all the joyous things from linking arms and bawling in happy unison that lively anthem of London's East End 'Knees up Mother Brown' – but they had forgotten that they were up to their calves in the un-yielding mud. They could no more lift their knees than could a man with wooden legs stuck in Plaster of Paris. Only the bobbing of their bodies up and down in time to the tune reminded one of the time

General Mark Clark

(Left) General Anders, commander of the Polish Corps in Italy

(Below) Mark Clark, Alexander and McCreery

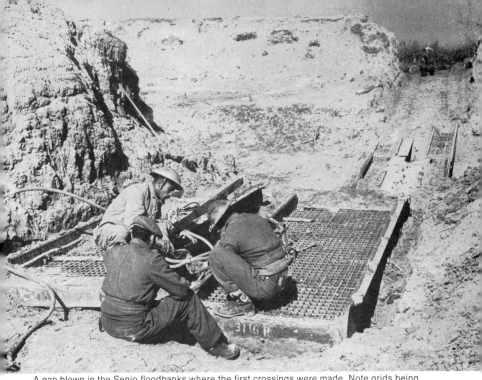

A gap blown in the Senio floodbanks where the first crossings were made. Note grids being positioned to enable heavy vehicles to get over. This picture was taken on 10th April 1945, some twenty-four hours afterwards. Dark specks on far bank were enemy machine gun positions.

A Sexton self-propelled gun crossing the Senio 10th April 1945. The bridge is made by a tank carrying its own bridge on top; observe the enormous two-storey flood banks.

Infantrymen racing against time to haul their assault boat over the Senio floodbank.

Germans surrendering with arms raised as they use a tiny footbridge pushed across by first wave of British assault troops. Note the narrow Senio compared with the formidable flood-banks.

honoured knee-knocking ritual and of the undeniable fact that while the spirit was willing the flesh, in the shape of their legs encased in concrete, was very weak indeed.

These were the times also when he indulged in the most precious personal activity of all, that of receiving and reading letters from home, and writing home himself. Every soldier will carry with him something of the agony and ecstasy brought about by the arrival of those little thin rectangular missives – namely the regulation air mail letters. Agony if there was nothing for him at all or if there was and it contained news of a love that was lost, of an infidelity, or perhaps of a bereavement. Ecstasy simply because there was a letter for him, and he knew he had not been forgotten. For security reasons all letters were censored and his family could not reveal much to him. So news was very sparse, very repetitive, and very humdrum. For the same reason his news to those back home was virtually non-existent. In this case the initial censorship was exercised by his own platoon commander who had to read the personal letters of his men which were all handed in unsealed. The fact that this never seemed to cause the slightest mutual embarrassment is quite extraordinary. The officer who regarded it as just another bloody chore would skim through the wording – inevitably as far as he was concerned a boring blend of love-laden and laboriously written banality. If he spotted anything like a place name or anything in the way of a fact or a figure which might conceivably be of help to the enemy he would simply scratch it out. He rarely if ever identified it with the author. In the same way the soldier saw the whole thing so impersonally that he was seldom if ever deterred from pouring out his love, his heart, and masses of kisses. In the many hundreds of letters, perhaps thousands of them, which it was my duty to read, not once did I detect any inhibition displayed by the writers because they knew that I or someone else would be reading them.

One would think that the close relationship between a small group of twenty to thirty men and their officer, when sensitive personal frictions and disciplinary considerations might cause difficulties, would open such censorship to abuse. The soldier would be hard put to it not to say something rude about his officer, and the officer might gain some unfair knowledge about the private life of his soldiers. Possibly somewhere somehow this may have happened but I have never heard of it. The fact that it could take place at all is a remarkable tribute to the civilised behaviour, integrity, and above all to the trust of both parties.

Another vastly important factor was the personal discipline undertaken by every soldier in keeping himself clean and observing the basic rules of 'field hygiene'. One may wonder what a 'field' had to do with it but this was just the Army's way of saying that one was out fighting and for the time being at least one had no fixed address. In these circumstances all written orders and dispatches had their place of origin tagged automatically as 'In the Field'. It conveyed both a romantic echo of campaigns long past and a rustic serenity which was hardly compatible with the reality. Nevertheless, the procedures and patterns of behaviour of the soldiers were recognised universally as being subject to special consideration whenever the word 'field' was used. For this reason every man was schooled to wash himself and have a good shave even when in spitting distance of the enemy.

Enormous care was taken virtually every minute of every day to ensure that anything which would attract flies was burnt or buried. There were few soldiers who by the end of the war had not suffered dysentery or some other fly-borne disease at one time or another, and each and every one had such a personal hatred of flies that there was never any need to remind him of evasive action. Garbage from the cookhouses and food 'left-overs' were buried as soon as possible. So were the dead, whether they were ours, the enemy, mules or other creatures. Latrines were dug deep and the protocols of rank were nearly always observed, those for officers being sited a safe distance from those provided for ordinary soldiers, presumably to enable their respective natural functions to be carried out without the mutual embarrassment of having to salute on the crouch with one's trousers down. Supplies of lime and reams of single sheet lavatory paper approximating in size, texture and colour to the neutral brown of the small sized emery paper, and referred to with mixed emotions as 'Army Form Blank' were liberally provided. Every unit had its 'Dan Dan the lavatory man'. He was the Sanitary Orderly who was responsible for maintaining and cleaning out latrines. Despite the unattractive nature of his job and its lack of prospects he was usually a most dedicated and revered figure in the battalion, enjoying a status normally accorded to the guru or the man who undeniably has a mission in life.

Latrine equipment in the field became quite sophisticated. Some units boasted three or four 'seaters' which could be placed over a narrow rectangular trench while resting on empty ammunition boxes. Virgin sandbags were then draped artistically between the seat and the ground to exclude the unsightly and above all to frustrate the fly. Further refinement of this friendly amenity if time permitted was the erection of a hessian screen all the way round and the provision of a small shovel (usually 'tool entrenching Mark I') with a heap of loose earth or sand, so that one could cover one's personal contribution to the next layer of the communal effort with a well directed consignment of dirt and dust. This was quite a tricky business, not only because it called for reasonable accuracy while only using one hand (the other being fully occupied with clutching paper and one's trousers at half-mast) but because it had to be done at high speed. One had roughly about five seconds between rising from one's seat, doing the shovelling, and closing the seat cover before the first fly arrived. Some flies were so crafty that they would alight surreptitiously behind one, quietly awaiting the lifting of one's posterior in order to gain admittance by making a quick dash for it. Consequently it was customary at all times to keep one's fly whisk at hand to carry out random sweeps behind one's back.

To observe three or four chaps going through all these movements at the same time but at different stages of their commitments – arriving, lowering trousers, fly whisking, sitting, grunting, fly whisking, rising, paper manipulating, shovelling, fly whisking, adjusting dress, and in between trying to read a letter from home or the *Eighth Army News*, was a very impressive experience. It is difficult to conceive of any situation more propitious for the individual to be able to demonstrate his ability to discharge so many disparate functions simultaneously.

A few like myself were the proud possessors of their own personal seat. Mine was a proper job which I found lying on the floor of a shattered house in a village which had been bombarded by both sides. Without wishing in any way to cast aspersions on the hygiene of the Italians it has to be said that it was very rare indeed for a water closet to be found anywhere except in the big houses and hotels of the major cities. So when I saw this nicely shaped wooden seat lying there I pounced on it and it was my constant companion for the rest of the war. When on the move I kept it behind the seat in my 'jeep' and as soon as we had occasion to stop for any length of time my devoted batman, Private Flynn, would dig the obligatory hole in a secluded area to a dimension which would allow a custom-built wooden box which he had made from the old 'compo' containers to be put over it. Then he would lift the seat reverently, place it carefully on top of the box, test the lid once or twice to see that it fitted snugly, and thus in a matter of minutes my throne was ready.

He did this so often that he got quite attached to the ritual. As a result and I do not know whether he was motivated by his regimental pride or his sense of humour, I suspect it was both, but the time came when he painted the regimental motto on the lid. This was '*Quid Nobis Ardui*', a Latin tag posing the rhetorical question in general terms 'what are dangers or difficulties to us?'

It was surprising how in practice, even under the most adverse conditions, the elementary rudiments of sanitation were achieved. It was only when one was actually in combat in the sense of being in direct contact with the enemy and under heavy fire that one had to dispense with the discipline in relieving oneself. Sometimes this had to be done within the confines of the slit trench simply because one was pinned down by enemy bombardment or the sniper's rifle. To try and stay alive, to sweat it out, to keep up one's courage, to continue to make some contribution to the military operation and its objective while being cooped up in a tiny slit trench and all the time being literally up to one's ankles in one's own stinking ordure for hours, even days, on end represent a confluence of agonies beyond the comprehension of any normal mortal except that of the infantryman who had to endure them.

Under such conditions it was impossible to shave, to have any change of clothing or to have any food except one's emergency ration consisting of a stick of chocolate as hard as a brick which one could only suck rather than chew. For water, precious water, one had permanently attached to one's equipment what looked like a jumbo size hip-flask. It was khaki-coloured and was fitted with a cork to stop the contents spilling which in turn was anchored to a stout piece of cord because without that cork not only would the water be lost but also the battle. Yet so marvellous were the disciplined reflexes of the well-trained and experienced soldier that within minutes of his having sufficient respite he would automatically clean himself up.

On one occasion when it was several degrees below zero and I was moving through a mountain pass at a point which only an hour before had been the outpost closest to the enemy, I saw a red-eyed sagging soldier of the Buffs sitting astride a pathetic little slit trench. He had taken off his boots and jacket so he was blue with cold. He had hung up his socks hopefully to dry which already bore the pearly stiffness of incipient icicles. He was jabbing a razor in frozen water nestling conveniently in the shell hole of what must have been a very 'near miss', and trying to shave himself. The places where he had hacked through the stubble were marked with spots of congealed blood. He had no mirror, but gazed instead in a mechanical sort of way into the middle distance. Fortunately, the horror and pain of it all was absorbed by the natural anaesthetic of a numbed face. Finally, to cap it all he set his defiance to music because I heard him humming through his chattering teeth a favourite cockney refrain of mine which with uncompromising lack of subtlety started its first verse with 'they're shifting father's grave to build a sewer'.

It was a curious fact of life during these war years that the soldier was quite unable to communicate with his colleagues without using language of the utmost profanity. It seemed that inside every soldier was a four letter word not only trying to get out, but actually doing so on every conceivable occasion. It emerged with the ease and regularity of a high security risk convict from an open prison. Fuck this and fuck that were so much part of every day parlance that not only was it used to punctuate nearly every word but on occasions when its utter banality through constant use was so frustratingly apparent the soldier would deploy it between syllables as well. Its introduction in this way for extra emphasis produced bizarre combinations.

This was vividly demonstrated on one occasion when we were having a hilarious sing-song at a company concert. Suitably fortified by a vino of such raw and recent vintage that the sediment still bore the footprints of the grape treaders, we started off with a subdued and somewhat emotional rendering of 'Me and My Girl'. Things started to warm up with 'hands knees and boomps a fucking daisy' and eventually were brought to a very boisterous climax when a dubious version of 'it's a long way to Tipperary' translated the unqualified farewell to London's famous landmark into 'Goodbye Picca fucking dilly'.

As Byrne Foxwell said, 'The language was something awful', but the natural mixture of the trite and the profane was perhaps in such abundance because without these ingredients how else could the soldier relate to his survival while keeping his sanity?

But while all this was going on during those miserable demoralising winter months which linked on one hand the pathetic end of 1944, a year of such high but squandered hopes, and on the other hand the sickening numbness and apathy of the early days of 1945 when the Italian campaign seemed doomed to suffocation under the pillow of its apparent unimportance and irrelevancy, bang in the middle of it all something happened which in less than three months produced what I contend was the most unlikely miracle in military history since David slew Goliath.

On 12th December 1944 General Alexander took over as Supreme Allied Commander, Mediterranean Forces and at the same time General Mark Clark moved up one to take Alexander's place as

Commander of the Fifteenth Army Group. This left a vacancy for command of Fifth (US) Army which was filled by General Lucien Truscott. The other army in the Fifteenth Army Group, the British Eighth Army, was at the time already commanded by Lieutenant-General Richard McCreery. Despite their personal philosophies and frictions, they all had for different reasons one great overriding and mutual motivation. Each one had still to prove something.

Alexander smarting from the frustration of his plans and doubtless irked privately by the spectacle of one of his former subordinates, General Montgomery, leading the assault in France, was determined somehow or other to show that he was not going to preside over a passive secondary role, or the dissolution of his plans to get to Vienna before the Russians did.

Mark Clark needed desperately to prove that he was a great commander. The discussion and debate attending his amphibious operations in general and his contentious capture of Rome in particular had conspired to rob him he felt of his due regard.

General Truscott who had been thrust fortuitously into the limelight at Anzio and who lived for so long in the shadow of Mark Clark whose style of command and handling of situations did not always fulfil Truscott's ultra professional criteria, was aching to remove any doubts about his own ability to practise with an army what first he had so clearly proved at divisional level.

Lieutenant General McCreery had perhaps the greatest personal ambition of them all. He had inherited the famous British Eighth Army whose line of brilliant commanders and unbroken successes since Alamein made it unthinkable that he should be the one to lead it shuffling into obscurity rather than marching to the matchless victory which its final days deserved.

All their aspirations could only be realised by one majestic and conclusive gamble. This was the battle for the River Po.

8. General Mark Clark

'Please leave out what I told you I did when
I was crossing the Po.'

GENERAL MARK CLARK

AT 7.30 a.m. on Thursday, 11th June 1964, I was awakened by the
telephone ringing in my bedroom. Groping for the receiver I was only
dimly aware that I was in Charleston, South Carolina, having spent
my first night in Hotel Fort Sumter.

'Welcome, Mr Harpur,' the voice said, 'It's General Clark. It would
be appreciated if you could be with me by eight o'clock because I am
planning to go out later to have a picnic with Mrs Clark. She is
convalescing after a serious operation and as it promises to be a very
hot day I want to take her up to the cool of the mountains.'

Somewhat awe-struck, because even if it were nearly twenty years
after the event, I was not exactly acclimatised to being spoken to direct
on the telephone by generals, especially one as legendary as Mark
Clark, I stood metaphorically to attention and said, 'Yessir'.

He was then the President of The Citadel which was the military
college of South Carolina and which, with Fort Sumter, had historic
connections with the very origins of the American Civil War a hundred
years earlier. He and I had corresponded at some length to set up the
meeting and I sensed that on learning of my choice of hotel he may have
used his influence to give me an impressive welcome from the outset,
because in a letter confirming the booking to my New York office
Mr Wesley W. Graves, the Manager, said 'Every courtesy will be
extended (including complimentary fruit in his room and flying the
British Flag) to assure Mr Harpur of a very pleasant visit with us.'
Never having had the Union Jack flown specifically in my honour
before I felt very important indeed.

As I hurriedly dressed, I rehearsed carefully the questions I was going to ask the General all of which I hoped would add up to the answers to the nagging questions I had in the deep recesses of my own mind for all these years. Why did he apparently frustrate Alexander's aims on the break-out from Anzio? What really made him go hell bent for Rome and neglect the complete destruction of the retreating German Tenth Army which would have ensured the fall of Rome anyway? How was it that at the end, despite all the doubts about both his personal prejudices and professional ability, he was able to conjure up a winning team from nothing? In short what manner of man was he? What made him tick?

The journey to the Citadel was but a short ride by taxi. Even at that hour of the morning the heat was uncomfortable. I noticed that some of the older negroes in the streets had already taken the protection of putting on ragged straw hats to cover their white locks. It was obviously going to be very hot indeed.

After passing through attractive streets of wooden walled houses with columns and verandas, set in gardens of flowers and creepers, which reminded one of some of the Hollywood sets for 'Gone with the Wind', I arrived at a large bungalow in the Citadel and paid off my taxi. There was a nice lady on the veranda setting out baskets of food who introduced herself as Mrs Clark.

'Oh you've come to the wrong place,' she said, 'the General is waiting for you in his office. He is so looking forward to meeting you because he loves, simply loves, talking about the war.' She gave me a warm smile and directions. Before an hour had passed she proved to be right. The General was talking his head off and treating me like an old buddy.

As I walked down a deserted minor road looking for the office, I saw a tall figure in the distance standing in the middle. He looked like a version of Gary Cooper waiting for a high noon shoot-out with the bad guy except that he had a more aquiline nose and a beguiling smile. There was no mistaking General Mark Clark. He advanced to meet me.

'Welcome,' he said 'I thought I would come out and look for you. In the maze of paths and roads people can get lost round here. Mrs Clark phoned down to say you were on your way. She has had one hell of an operation. Part of her artery system has been replaced by tubes made of Dacron,' he confided.

Considerably encouraged by this warm and informal greeting, and having expressed the usual good wishes for Mrs Clark's recovery, I said as we reached the door of his office, 'You know, General, this is the second time I have followed you a very long way.' Before I could go on he said somewhat puzzled 'What was the first one?'

'All the way up Italy from Taranto to Turin,' I replied.

He beamed. It seems I could not have made a more happy first impression. He put his hand upon my shoulder. 'We have a lot to talk about. Come on in and make yourself comfortable.'

Inside his beautifully air-conditioned office I noticed immediately that he had surrounded himself, perhaps not surprisingly, with innumerable items relating directly or indirectly to his many achievements. There was a large impressive desk flanked by three flags including 'Old Glory'. On the front of the desk was a nameplate inscribed in large letters 'General Mark W. Clark, Commanding General'. On the walls were pictures of Mark Clark including a whole group depicting various shots of the final surrender in Italy. On a side table there was a gigantic album containing a vast number of pictures of his days with the Fifth US Army and Fifteenth Army Group. On the wall facing his desk was a photograph of Eisenhower. Naturally one would assume this to be simple evidence of Mark Clark's friendship not only for a brother in arms but for one who also wrote the preface to Mark Clark's book *Calculated Risk*. I was to discover before the morning was out that this overt tribute to 'Ike' was most misleading.

We sat opposite each other in comfortable chairs. I put my camera and notebook on my lap and waited. He picked up a letter I had sent to him, glanced over it quickly, and fixing me with a piercing eye he said, 'I understand you are only interested in material for the London *Evening News* about the final battles in Italy.'

I assured him that although I was not a journalist this was in fact the main reason for my visit, although I hoped he would not mind if we discussed other aspects of the Italian campaign as well.

'Such as what?' he asked.

I knew it would be fatal if I were to impale him straightaway on the barbs of some of the blunt and embarrassing questions I had already rehearsed. We had only met for ten minutes. Somehow I had to find a way of gaining his confidence. Necessity in this case was the mother of an inspired intervention. Before I could answer the telephone rang. He went over to his desk, picked up the receiver, and carried on a conversation about a draft of young boys which was shortly expected to arrive at the Citadel for summer camp. The problem of the ones likely to be homesick appeared to concern him.

In the precious minute that ensued I tried to think of a question which would both please him and open the gateway to a truly revealing discussion about the man himself. The enigma of Mark Clark, the man who in the opinion of some might have shortened the war by a year if he had held fast to Alexander's directive at Anzio, and who in the end brought the Italian campaign to a seemingly impossible victory, had to be solved. It appears presumptuous, even ridiculous, that I an ordinary civilian and once a very ordinary temporary soldier, should take it upon myself to manoeuvre this meeting after all those years in order to check him out for myself. Yet there I was, and I was determined not to waste a second of this unique opportunity. I know my introductory question would set the tone of our conversation and it was one which I had not properly thought out.

He came back to his chair. As he sat down he said, 'I hope you did not mind me calling you so early this morning and that your hotel is comfortable.' I reassured him on both points but as he mentioned the hotel the vision of their flying the British flag in my honour flashed across my mind. Whether it was this or some hidden thought deep down in my subconscious which prompted me, but the next thing I knew I was blurting out a question which in the parlance of rocketry gave our dialogue superb first time lift-off.

'General Clark,' I said – having read Dale Carnegie's book *How to win friends and influence people* I knew the value of repeating the subject's name – 'I believe that you have never been given full credit for your achievement in the final offensive in Italy.' He perked up. In fact he leant forward slightly. 'For example you had the problems of handling contingents from many different nations. While these are understandable by reason alone of differences of language, religion, national characteristics and customs, tell me quite frankly what you really thought of the British?'

He raised his eyebrows, 'Why do you ask that? You must know from the record that I thought the British were great.'

'The reason I asked it,' I said, 'was because the Eighth Army and other troops from the United Kingdom represented, apart from the Americans, your biggest force and it was obviously most important that you should get on well with them all. Did they not irritate you in some way?' He pondered on this for a few seconds. Obviously the sympathetic emphasis I gave to my last few words made him relax.

'You know, Mr Harpur,' – obviously he had read Dale Carnegie too – 'I probably knew the British better than they knew themselves. I was closer to them than even Ike. He never had to live in a submarine with them as I did, and believe me there is no better way of getting to know people than being cooped up with them under the water.'

He took it for granted, quite rightly, that I had read of his being taken in His Majesty's submarine *Seraph* on a clandestine mission to meet up with French military leaders prior to the Allied invasion of Algeria in November 1942. But it was his gratuitous almost snide reference to General Eisenhower that first gave me an inkling of the pent-up conflicts of the man.

'I doubt if he ever had the careful counsel and advice as I had about the origins and philosophy of the British and their Common-wealth which enabled me to understand them better than any other American. My greatest tutor was your Sir John Dill when he was heading the British Mission in Washington. No man knew more about the whole of the British set-up and their different traditions and attitudes than he did. He and men like Sir Ronald Adam, the Adjutant-General of your Army Council and for whom I have the highest respect helped me enormously. They made me understand the supreme importance to the British following their disastrous casualties in two World Wars of conserving manpower. I think this sometimes made them too damn cautious.'

He paused. 'Like at the Volturno,' I interjected helpfully. In October 1943 this river crossing south of Rome when McCreery commanding the British X Corps had a row with Mark Clark about the plan which appeared to expose the British to excessive casualties, was I felt what he had in mind.

'Was it the Volturno or the Garigliano river crossing?' he reflected more by way of surprise than as a direct question. 'Come to think of it I believe it was both. We Americans tend to be what I would call 'broad front' men. In going over a river we like to attack all along the line more or less simultaneously in the expectation that the enemy will be confused as to where our real punch will lie, even though we may only be guessing at that ourselves, and when we have probed where the enemy's weakness lies then we bring up our reserves and go through there. The British tend to concentrate a jab at one point or two alone, and then only after a big build up of preparations beforehand with all the supporting arms and firepower they can muster. This could and did lead to excessive delays. So I and Dick McCreery, who I can tell you was a damn fine general, had opposing philosophies. He some-times felt that my 'broad front' plan called for too many risks, too much waste of resources, and above all unnecessary casualties. We had serious disagreements about it. On one occasion he was so upset that I had to walk him out into the middle of a field so that we could have a man to man talk out of earshot of his staff officers. It is very bad for commanders to be seen to be disagreeing.

'On another occasion he argued with Al Gruenther, my Chief of Staff, about our attack being badly planned and that he for one was not going to commit his troops on a suicide course. He was going to stop his part of the operations. I had to go off right away and nail him on the spot. "What's all this, Dick, about the attack being off?" I asked him. I could see he was very angry because he looked at me with a real glint in his eye and he said very coldly, "That is quite right. Your Chief of Staff knows all about it." He did not seem to want to discuss it any more and I had the hell of a job to get him straightened out. I explained to him that all the formations were going into action on the basis of my plan and although he didn't like it my orders simply had to be accepted. "You know, Dick," I said, "each of us at times is told to do things we do not like but we are soldiers and we have to do them. Orders are orders." It was typical of Dick McCreery that as soon as he got things off his chest he would make it quite clear that once the decision was taken he would co-operate one hundred per cent. He never let me down.'

As if by some subsconscious direction our conversation was veering quite naturally to the fundamental issue of the giving and taking of orders. This gave me the opening for which I had waited twenty years.

'General Clark, have you, like General McCreery, ever felt the need to disobey an order and if so what did you do about it?' I asked. He sat motionless and for a moment I wondered if the directness of my question had upset him. I need not have worried for within the minute he was replying with considerable animation and most articulately, as if he were at pains to spell the whole thing out for me.

'I believe that you should obey orders implicitly as long as you feel that they are well-founded. I suppose that any great commander at one time or another has faced the necessity of disobeying an order for this reason but being a great commander he probably contrived to do so on some pretext which got both him and the people giving the order off the hook. The perfect example of this of course is Nelson and his "blind eye".'

At this point I interrupted him, 'But, General, if what you say is true then as you certainly rank as a great commander you must have some personal experience of turning your own blind eye.'

He looked at me thoughtfully. He was obviously flattered and the question intrigued him. I got the distinct impression he was searching in vain for some occasion which would demonstrate that in common with other great commanders he too had conformed to his definition of insubordination. Surely now was the time to prompt him about his extraordinary behaviour over the capture of Rome. I took the bull by the horns. 'One possible instance I had in mind, General, was when you changed the direction of your attack in the break-out from Anzio and instead of following the line laid down apparently by Alexander himself to cut off completely the German Tenth Army you suddenly switched towards Rome.'

General Clark drew himself up in his chair. God, I thought to myself, he is going to fling me out. But no. He leant forward instead and tapping my pad with his index finger he said quite gently, 'Take a note of this, because there has been more nonsense written about that damned incident than anything else I ever did. The fact is that I fulfilled my mission. It may interest you to know that in a way I was over-conscientious in carrying it out because my Commander-in-Chief told me that above all else Rome had to be captured before the invasion of Normandy began and the Americans, not the British, were to do it. My Commander-in-Chief was the President himself, the late President Roosevelt.'

This strange twist astonished me. 'But, surely,' I said to him, 'your commander was General Alexander and you admit in your own book *Calculated Risk* that he was insisting all along on your using your forces in the first instance to cut off the German lines of communication at Valmonte. Did you not have qualms about whom to acknowledge and about frustrating Alexander's intentions?'

General Clark sat back. Tall, handsome and very dignified he cut a magnificent figure as he contemplated me. I felt like a ragged private soldier being inspected closely by the first Duke of Wellington. In view of the critical line our conversation was now taking I could be excused for thinking once again that this time he really would throw me out. But he could not have been nicer.

'It must be very confusing for you,' he replied 'and I am grateful to you for coming all this way to find out first hand, because how I saw it is quite different from how it has been interpreted by people who never met me in their life. The facts are that everybody agreed including Churchill and Alexander months before the event, that Rome was the primary objective. Alexander never gave me orders not to take Rome. He never really gave me any orders to do anything because he always talked things over with me and after taking my views into account we would more or less agree a course of action. But actual *orders*–never. I know he was concerned about my maintaining my thrust to Valmonte, but hell when we were knocking on its door we had already destroyed as much of the German Tenth Army as we could ever have expected. By this time I learnt that Alexander was questioning my intentions through my own Chief of Staff and it looked as if he wanted to run my own Goddam army without ever talking to me man to man. One thing I knew was that *I* had to take Rome and that my American army was going to do it. So in all the circumstances I had to go for it before the British loused it up.'

He paused for a second and feeling perhaps that he had overstepped the mark he added, 'Don't get me wrong, I am not being critical of the British because they are the best people in the world to have on your side, it was just that my determination to take Rome was so great, I did not want any accident of planning or interference from Alexander's staff to stop me taking Rome. We Americans had slogged all the way up from Salerno and I was not going to have this great prize, the honour of taking Rome, denied to me and my GI's by anyone. We had earned it, you understand.'

I nodded as understandingly as I could. It was obvious to me that the honour of taking Rome meant far more to him than I had ever imagined. As if reading my thoughts, and he probably was, he went on, 'It was very important indeed that Rome should fall before the D-Day landings in Normandy to give the invasion a boost and I did it with no more than about a day to spare. I did it,' he repeated with slightly greater emphasis on the 'I'. Then as if by way of increasing my general knowledge and with a very modest manner which did not conceal from me the real clue to his motivation and character he added, 'You may like to know for the record, Mr Harpur, in case you did not know it already, that since history began the number of commanders who achieved the capture of Rome from the south could be numbered on the fingers of only one hand – probably less, and I am one of them.'

No man gets to the top without some mixture of ambition and conceit and the thought flashed into my mind that for Mark Clark the capture of Rome pandered to both in the highest degree. But I argued inwardly surely he as a thoroughly professional soldier would not throw away the guarantee of the complete destruction of an enemy army just to satisfy a personal and selfish ambition. I needed more evidence that this conjecture could be true, and about two hours later he gave himself away in the most unexpected manner. But first my reverie was interrupted by his saying :

'I still have not answered your question about my having an occasion when I disobeyed an order, so I will tell you about one. General

Marshall, who next to the President was our most important commander, came to visit me near Florence in the spring of 1945. Normally
one provides a special guard of honour to greet important visitors on
such occasions but he ordered me not to do so this time. He was quite
adamant about it. Just the same I lined up a small squad from about
twenty different units representing most of the different nationalities
who came under my Fifteenth Army Group. When the General stepped
off the plane he snapped at me, 'I thought I said no honours' but I
persuaded him to make a tour of inspection. Afterwards he was very
pleased because otherwise he might never have realised fully what an
enormous and complex command I had.'

I was aware already of this incident from Mark Clark's book in
which he gave a much more detailed account than he gave me but both
versions left me in no doubt that Mark Clark, while undoubtedly
dramatising the nature of his command to secure General Marshall's
co-operation in getting the support he wanted, was also just plain
'showing off'. He had a flair for showmanship and self-publicity, which,
let us face it, often goes hand in hand with people who get things done,
not the least being Bernard Law Montgomery.

We then settled into a detailed discussion of the countless problems,
and personalities relating to the battle for the River Po. It flowed easily.
I was able to take note after note in quick succession without disturbing
him, so great was his enthusiasm and concentration. He had a gift of
painting the broad picture at each stage and being able to go back to
add a vivid little re-touch in the shape of an anecdote or other personal
aside, yet never losing the theme. It became clear that for this battle
anyway he was no longer a 'broad front' man and above all although
as he put it 'Bologna was the prize' the total destruction of the German
forces came first. What caused this change in the man who originally
opposed McCreery and Alexander on analagous issues? In the later
chapters which I devote to the battle itself the reasons will become clear.

Then at his invitation we went through his enormous album of
photographs which took up a prominent position on a long table next
the wall. As he flicked over the pages he gave me a brief verbal caption
for each picture. It was apparent that whatever the occasion, even when
up in the forward battle areas, he always seemed to be lucky enough
to have a photographer at hand. It would be naive to assume that this
was just a coincidence. In fact it was well-known that he regarded his
entourage as never being complete without a good complement of war
correspondents and photographers. His inability to resist a topical news
peg on which to hang his own ego was immediately demonstrated even

in the unlikely ambience of going through some old photographs with a nobody like myself. He came to one page which had a large picture showing a whole group of officers standing in rows behind each other. He was seated in the middle in the front and around him was this mass of faces resembling the traditional end of term school photograph.

He went on to explain, 'This is a picture of all my staff officers at my Fifteenth Army Group Headquarters. Apart from me and my very senior officers sitting in the front do you recognise any of the others?' I scanned the faces row by row trying to spot somebody like Eisenhower or Alexander or even Clark Gable who might have slipped in unnoticed. As the faces were only about half the size of a postage stamp I could be excused if I was a little slow in identifying anybody. Suddenly he put his finger on a face about the fifth row back. This was not so much a gesture of impatience as one of suppressed excitement.

'Take a look at that one,' he commanded. 'Do you know who he is?' Still I failed to register. It was probably General McCreery or Harold MacMillan or even Winston Churchhill I thought to myself and doubt-less there was a good story about why one of them had turned up in this improbable position. Completely baffled I had to admit that the face meant nothing to me. 'That,' he said tapping the face several times during which he paused for some seconds, undoubtedly to increase the dramatic effect, 'is none other than John Profumo.'

I was somewhat shocked not so much by the disclosure but because of my subconscious reaction to the need for Mark Clark to single out this individual. I suppose it was a natural thing to do because the so-called John Profumo–Christine Keeler scandal had not long elapsed but it was the way in which Mark Clark brought it up in isolation when there must have been countless others in the same photograph who for one reason or another were or were to become famous or infamous as the case may be, that made me feel that he derived a strange satisfaction from the unexpected publicity which the ricochet of the scandal gave him. I had the good fortune to meet John Profumo on two fleeting occasions in later years when I found, as so many will testify, that he is a very nice, modest, and remarkable person. I mentioned this incident to him and we both had a good chuckle over it.

When we had got to the end of the album I realised that the General had come to a decision. He was not going to conclude our interview as he might well have done. Instead he put his hand on my shoulder and giving it a gentle shake he said, 'You know, Brian, I feel you and I are getting along just fine, why don't you stay a little longer? Come back to my home and I will show you some more and we'll continue our chat there.' I felt enormously flattered. We had already been over an hour together and here he was now not only putting me on christian name terms but seeking to prolong our acquaintance.

As we walked back to his house I remember vividly snatches of his replies to the somewhat aimless and wide ranging questions I asked by way of conversation.

In view of his experience in commanding so many different nationalities in Italy and subsequently in the Korean war what did he think of a permanent United Nations peace-keeping force?

'I am very pessimistic about the United Nations ever being united. Who would command such a force? Who could they find who would match for example my own proven ability and experience? I say again "who would command"? There would be too many little nations. Too many tugs in different directions. . . . They would have no undisputed leader to comand them whom they would respect.'

What did he think was the most important attribute of a man called upon to lead an army? 'There is no question about that at all. Given that he is a professional in the art of warfare it is his own personal magnetism and power of personal leadership. This must go hand in hand with his ability to communicate, to see that his orders are carried out. I had my own small aeroplane. I called it my "cub", so that I could fly all over the place to meet my commanders who were often hundreds of miles apart and to explain to them exactly what they had to do. I had landing strips made at all my Divisional Headquarters. Mind you, I was very impressed with the British system of once having decided upon a plan of getting everybody down the line put in the picture.'

Bearing in mind he was now in South Carolina where there was a high proportion of black population did he think the soldiers of negro origin were any better or worse than their white counterparts?

'Funny you should ask because I have just been in trouble over that. It so happens I was the first to have an all black division in the Fifth US Army in Italy. Now here was a formation composed entirely of black Americans, and commanded by black officers, and I can tell you the first time the Germans came at them they ran like hell. It was a poor show. However, you must remember that they had responsibilities put upon them which the nature of their treatment and existence in this country did not fit them for. It was not their fault. When they pulled themselves together they did some good work. As a matter of fact just recently I said some things in a speech which were taken as being derogatory about the military worth of our black boys and there was the hell of a row. I had to get my speech suppressed.

'Fortunately, I have got a great friend, a newspaper editor here called 'Red' Hitt and he helped me to sort it out. Otherwise I think I would have been lynched. Frankly, the average black soldier by the very nature of his attitude could never be as good as the average white one but in due course as he becomes more independent and better educated all that will change.'

By this time we had reached General Mark Clark's residence. It was a large comfortable bungalow-style construction and he took me straight into his study. Occupying every bit of space on walls, desk, tables and cabinets were tributes in one form or another to Mark Clark. There was a striking portrait of him on his horse apparently by Annigoni. Rows of medals, orders, insignia including his honorary knighthood from King George VI were on display. Plaques and other reproductions of his various corps and army signs were there en masse. I was staggered. I felt I had walked into a shrine which would have put one even dedicated to Napoleon to shame. There was no doubt that Mark Clerk loved to be surrounded by, I am tempted to say buried in, every bit of the memorabilia which drew attention to his achievements and to which he could draw the attention of others.

He pointed out to me a stunning picture of Queen Elizabeth II, the medal of Grand Officer of the Legion of Honour presented to him by General Charles de Gaulle, and the Order of Suvorov first class, which was the highest army decoration given to anyone outside the Soviet Union. He then picked up a framed letter to him from Churchill which in simple pithy Churchillian phrases urged Mark Clark to make the best possible use of the landing craft for the Anzio operation so that they could then be released quickly to return to Britain.

'You know, Brian, I prize this letter more in some ways than these other things,' he waved his hand vaguely indicating the countless objects in other parts of the room, 'because here was your great, great Churchill reposing his confidence in me and taking the trouble to write to me personally. You see, Churchill had to fight like hell to keep the landing craft from going back for the Normandy invasion before we could use them at Anzio. There was a shortage of these vital craft and if Eisenhower had been allowed to have his way they would have been rusting in England months before they were needed and my plans to capture Rome would have been killed. Churchill and I were both in this together and I can tell you never have I appreciated a letter more.'

There was something about the way he identified himself with Churchill, almost as if they were equals, and in the way he referred to Eisenhower which to my surprise was one of undisguised contempt that caused me to ask slightly flippantly 'Do I gather that on this occasion Eisenhower was not entirely on your side?' Mark Clark went over to the window, looked thoughtfully outside for a few seconds and without turning round uttered several short sentences in a flat clinical monotone which accentuated the intensity which prompted them.

'I doubt if Eisenhower was ever entirely on anybody's side at any time. I doubt if he had the capacity to identify which side he ought to be on even if he wanted to be on somebody's side. Ike was not a soldier. He was a politician. He was a fence-sitter. He was the great compromiser. He was not a professional. He was not a soldier, he was just a compromiser.'

I could hardly believe my ears. Here was General Mark Clark dismissing the Supreme Commander, the beloved and inspirational 'Ike', the man whom Mark Clark presumably invited to write the foreword to his own book *Calculated Risk* and in which Mark Clark paid tribute to Ike's great qualities, and whose portrait hung in Mark Clark's office in The Citadel, in terms which now clearly belied this apparent respect. Indeed there was no mistaking the real scorn he had for Eisenhower. This lay deep-seated beneath the veneer of a relationship which one would have deemed to have been good until one appreciated, not without justification that Mark Clark in his book had very little good to say about Ike unless it was by way of Ike saying something good about him. Before I could delve further into this antipathy which possibly was compounded by jealousy and conceit – after all Mark Clark at 46 was the youngest three-star general in the history of the United States and it must have been galling for him to see someone like Eisenhower without his professional qualifications or combat experience rocketing to glory above him – I was diverted by his adding, 'Mind you, Eisenhower was probably the only one who could have handled this job.' Ah, I thought to myself he is going to make amends and put the record straight. Unfortunately, the sting in the tail removed for ever any doubt in my mind about his disdain when he concluded with 'Because no one with any strong views of his own or professionalism would take it on. Only a born compromiser could get away with it.'

We went on chatting away. He told me how shortly he was going to Brazil for a reunion of some of the Brazilian Expeditionary Force one of the thirty nations who fought in Italy. He was obviously pleased and proud to be their guest of honour. Another nice trait he revealed was his description of how he managed to get over a hundred soldiers from the Polish Corps a job in Argentina. I was saddened to hear that not only did he have a very sick wife, but his daughter had died suddenly only two years previously. He pointed out to me with justifiable pride a portrait of his only son, Major William Doran Clark (also a graduate of West Point and wounded in Korea) which had been painted by his daughter. I sensed as we looked at this picture that now we had reached such informal almost intimate acquaintance the time had come for me to go before something spoilt it. He had been charming and courteous throughout and I wanted to take away with me something which would characterise a most happy memory of my visit.

'General,' I said, 'you have given me the privilege of quite a few hours of your conversation and companionship and I would like to take a picture of you in some setting or with something in your hand with which you think you would like to be best remembered. What about holding the insignia of Honorary Knight of the British Empire, or the Order of Suvorov, or a copy of *Calculated Risk* or something like that?' I suggested. He looked at me for what seemed like a whole minute.

'I do not know if this is what you have in mind but there is only one thing, one thing alone, for which I hope you will best remember me and you might like to photograph me with that. It is something I have not shown you yet and few people have ever seen it.' Considerably mystified I followed him out on to a patio at the back of the house. As he emerged he turned around and I saw that he was pointing to what was obviously a large directional sign. It was the sort of sign one would see prominently displayed at a major road junction giving the distance to some large city. It was long, rectangular and had what looked like a bullet hole near one edge. It was slightly faded, but the letters were unmistakeable being picked out in reflector dots. They spelt out 'ROMA'.

'I captured this when I was on the brink of entering the Eternal City, it's a souvenir that means more to me than all the other things I had given to me or collected.' In a flash I now knew for certain that the taking of Rome was far more important to him than obeying Alexander's expressed intention, while not explicit order, to destroy completely the Tenth German Army. Sensing that I was now in a unique position to take what could truly be an historic picture, certainly one which in the context of our conversation could never be so revealing, I carefully aimed my camera at him and the sign and prayed that this snap would come out. It did. I could see that he was immensely gratified to be photographed next to the one thing which in a long professional career meant more emotionally to him than any of the other honours and distinctions which had been heaped upon him.

'They can't take that achievement away from you,' I said pointing to the 'ROMA' sign.

'Well, a lot of people have had a damn good try,' he replied, 'but now I am getting old, I'm not so explosive. But to be first into Rome, that was really something.'

He then arranged for one of his senior staff at The Citadel, a Colonel Hoy, to give me a conducted tour : 'Don't forget to show Mr Harpur the British territory which I command on this campus,' he instructed him and then turning to me he said, 'It's been a real pleasure to have you with me this day, Brian. You are quite right. That last battle in Italy was an amazing one. Probably one of the most extra-ordinary battles ever fought. Don't forget all I told you about how we won, but perhaps you could gloss over that incident about what I did when I was halfway across the Po,' he smiled. 'If you do I will send you a copy of my battle orders to the Fifteenth Army Group for this final attack from the official records of the Department of the United States Army.'

Actually I did not gloss over that incident to which he referred as will be seen later on but I did get his battle orders just the same.* He could not resist sending them to me because Mark Clark wanted to be quite certain that this evidence of his imprimatur on what was arguably his own greatest personal achievement, far bigger than the capture of Rome, was in my hands. We said goodbye on the veranda and he went about the business of the picnic for his wife which had been delayed far far longer than either of us had anticipated by virtue of our long discussion.

Colonel Hoy, a dapper alert and sparely built man wearing a simple white shirt with dark tie and a pair of slacks, put on his sun glasses and said, 'Let's go and have a look at the General's British territory.' We walked briskly on to the parade ground and there at one corner was a conical-shaped white edifice open at the sides, and with a dark pencil like object sticking like a spike out of the top. 'This,' said Colonel Hoy, 'is one of the General's most prized souvenirs. It is the periscope of the British Navy's submarine *Seraph* which nominally under the American flag took the General on his secret mission to meet the French generals before the invasion of North Africa. It is the only place where the Royal Navy's White Ensign is allowed by your Admiralty to fly on shore.' He then went on to show me the 'Mark Clark' Hall in the lobby in which were twelve flags beautifully encased.

'These,' said Colonel Hoy, 'are another prized possession of the

* See Appendix A.

General. They are the flags of some of the nations and formations in
the Italian Campaign which General Clark requested be sent to him
at that time, so that when he was visited officially in Italy by very
important people like the late President Roosevelt and other Heads of
State he could have them flown in their honour.'

I wondered if Colonel Hoy knew that in the patio of the General's
own home he had a souvenir which he valued even more than these
not inconsiderable prizes. But I decided not to mention the 'Roma' sign.
There was no point.

As I returned to my hotel I pondered upon General Clark, the
'American Eagle' as Churchill dubbed him, and I could see him standing there proudly beside that reminder of what in his own estimation
put him alongside the greatest commanders of the past. His words 'to
be first into Rome, that was really something' echoed in my mind. His
obsession with his long cherished ambition had undoubtedly affected his
judgement in the crucial break-out from Anzio. Whatever justification
he claimed the fact came through crystal clear that he had let Alexander
down. The latter in his memoirs said, not I suspect without a hint of
bitterness :

> I had always assumed General Clark in conversation that Rome
> would be entered by his Army; and I can only assume that the
> immediate lure of Rome for its publicity value persuaded him to
> switch the direction of his advance.

It was not until over thirty years later that I learnt of an incident
which robbed Mark Clark of his claim that only he and his Americans
were first into Rome. Lunching in the Garrick Club in London with
Sir Geoffrey Cox, that distinguished journalist, author, and founder
of ITN (Britain's famed Independent Television News Service), I
mentioned to him my belief that Mark Clark had an obsession amount-
ing to paranoia about getting to Rome first. Sir Geoffrey said, 'Indeed,
I can give you first-hand knowledge. I was in Italy at the time serving
with the New Zealand Corps, and when it was obvious that Rome
was about to fall General Freyberg ordered me to get to the Vatican
as fast as possible where his son who had been a prisoner was believed
to have found sanctuary. Armed with suitable messages and credentials
from General Freyberg to enlist General Mark Clark's sympathies and
assistance, I duly presented myself at his Fifth Army HQ. I was wearing
the British Eighth Army flash on my shoulder and I have no doubt
that because of this instead of being speeded on my way I was ordered
not to go forward at all. They did not want anybody from the Eighth

Army to have the opportunity of getting into Rome at the same time as the Americans did. I was virtually held prisoner!'

However, Sir Geoffrey with that resourcefulness which characterised his setting up of ITN and other achievements was not going to be beaten. He explained to the suspicious American staff officers that reluctantly he had to accept the situation but surely they would not mind if while he was waiting he had his jeep filled up with petrol. They agreed. Sir Geoffrey then instructed his driver that when he went outside the camp to get the petrol he was not to return. Instead he fixed up a rendezvous well outside the perimeter where they would meet at dawn.

'There was I,' said Sir Geoffrey, 'at the appointed time moving about like a Red Indian in order to avoid the American sentries and security patrols, and I got clear away. I met up with my driver and as a result I was certainly among the first into the Eternal City.'

9. General Sir Richard McCreery

'I only had two problems. One was Mark Clark,
the other was how to get an army over a river
which was so narrow in places that even a one-legged
man could jump it.'

GENERAL MCCREERY

It was precisely 6.30 pm on Tuesday, 16th February 1965, that at the invitation of General Sir Richard McCreery I presented myself at the Cavalry Club in London. He was awaiting me. He gave no hint of the strain he was under because I learnt later that the next day he was flying out to New Zealand to be at the bedside of his eldest son who was very seriously ill. Earlier he had written to me from Somerset saying : 'I shall be very pleased to discuss with you the final stages of the Italian Campaign, and the part played by the Eighth Army in the final Po offensive.' He was better than his word. He took enormous trouble to go through the whole complex operation point by point and appreciating that although one does not flash papers around in prestigious London clubs I might like to make a surreptitious note or two, he found me a quiet corner where sitting side by side in the privacy of a large cavernous couch I was able to do so.

As I took stock of him I could not help but feel instantly the natural dignity and authority of a great gentleman who happened also to become a truly great professional soldier. Educated at Eton and Sandhurst he joined the 12th Lancers in 1915 and served in France in the 1914–1918 war. It so happened that his regiment was one of the first to be mechanised and consequently he obtained long experience of armoured warfare. Indeed after fighting through the Dunkirk debacle in 1940 his aptitude was fortunately recognised. He was made up to acting major-general and as one of the comparatively young, energetic and progressive generals he was entrusted with the organising and training of new armoured divisions. Subsequently he was sent to the Middle East in 1942 in the expectation that his considerable expertise in armoured warfare would help to reorganise the Eighth Army's unsuccessful tactics. He was never brought in at a level where his advice could be properly evaluated and put into action. A clue to the character of the man is that he became so adamant in opposing some of the proposals for the future use of the armoured formations that he was sacked. He was not afraid to stand up and be counted for the things he believed in, even though it could mean sacrificing his career. Fortunately, just as he was kicking his heels in Cairo awaiting his unhappy return to England, there was a change at the top. General Alexander arrived to take over the Middle East command from General Auchinleck.

As he went around his HQ he found Richard McCreery alone in a room without a job and promptly made him his Chief of Staff. Alexander and McCreery had fought alongside each other at Dunkirk. They saw eye to eye with each other. They were trusted friends. Thus was forged a link which was to last from then onwards to the end of the war. Their rapport when Alexander was Supreme Commander of the Mediterranean theatre and McCreery Commander of the Eighth Army had a decisive influence on Mark Clark in the planning of the battle for the Po.

In the quiet atmosphere of the Cavalry Club it did not take long to relax and to put our feet up, as it were, on the footstool of mutual memories and experiences shared. After enquiring with genuine interest about my own unremarkable army career, Sir Richard took the initiative with a direct question which carried us right into the heart of the events we had met to discuss. 'Tell me,' he said, 'how was your encounter with Mark Clark?' I had mentioned to him in a letter about my visit to Charleston and obviously this had aroused his curiosity. I gave him a full account including the incidents in which they both appeared to have had severe disagreements.

When I had finished he sat in silence for a while and nodding his head gently. 'There is no denying,' he said, 'that on occasions I had terrific arguments with Mark Clark on some of his battle plans because I thought they would cause quite unnecessary loss of life. As you know, one of the principles of warfare is concentration, the ability to bring together sufficient force at the right time to give the enemy a good old knock on the chin. Mark Clark was often too keen to probe the enemy's defences over such a wide area in order to find their weak spot that by the time he had found it countless lives had been thrown away, and the ability to find reserves to exploit such knowledge so expensively gained was impaired. There are other ways of determining the enemy's dispositions without having to resort to brute force in the first place. I hated the waste of human lives and of our precious resources in any form or manner. I hated it. I hated it.'

I sat riveted to my seat as this handsome dignified man infected me with the intensity of his feeling without his having to make a single inflection or gesture to emphasise a point. In a quiet, almost deferential, conversational voice which somehow underlined his conviction he continued, 'When I said there were other ways of finding out the best place to concentrate one's major effort in attack, I do not deny that at the end of the day one still has to use brute force. But in that event it should be used with discretion with the enemy's weak points already in mind and not just as an exercise of reconnaissance in force in the hope that something favourable will turn up. This is particularly true of river crossings where one had to make sure that one's troops were not exposed over long on the wrong side in full view of the enemy and his very considerable fire power. I did all I could to prevent this sort of thing becoming a blood bath.' He paused for a few seconds as if wondering why he had allowed this alliterative cliché to escape in what was otherwise a simple matter of fact explanation of his philosophy.

'Do you think then that Mark Clark tended to take the "blood bath" approach rather than the other ways you mentioned?' I interjected. He considered this for a few seconds. 'I think if I pursue that question I might be on dangerous ground. Let me put it this way. Mark Clark, who I can assure you has as many fine qualities as any man bearing great responsibilities is entitled to have, indeed has to have, was just as concerned as I was about keeping casualties down, but on occasions his methods were not my methods and I honestly believe that if he had then followed my advice not only would many lives have been saved but we would have had more success in breaking through the enemy's defences. The key to everything in battle is so simple really. This is what you must have.'

He leant forward slightly and started to count them off on his fingers. 'One, you must have good intelligence and I mean that,' he added with just the hint of a twinkle,' in every sense of the word, and I will explain more about that later. Two, you must have good organisation – your troops must be well trained, well supplied, and well motivated. Three, you must always have up your sleeve an enormous element of surprise because this can fox the enemy, give you the initiative, save lives, and provide an unforeseen bonus which is up to you to identify and exploit before it disappears. Four – you must never give the enemy any rest. Never let him rest. Always be doing something to which he has to re-act. If you don't then he'll be doing something to which you have to re-act and you have lost the initiative. No, never let him rest. And I mean that literally as well. A soldier has to sleep sometimes so if you have a machine gun or mortar crew or a small team manning just one gun of the Royal Artillery and you say to them 'Listen, chaps, go well back behind the lines and get some good sleep during the day because you are going to come forward at dusk and be up all night making sure the enemy gets no sleep" they will only be too pleased to oblige. You can imagine the effect upon the enemy trying to get some sleep when a mortar bomb keeps exploding at frequent but irregular intervals in his area, especially if it's a nice big noisy one. A soldier who gets little or no sleep becomes demoralised and useless. No, never let them rest. Keep their High Command twitching about your next move and don't let even one of their soldiers have a good night's sleep.' He paused.

'Did not Mark Clark subscribe to the same formula?' I asked.

Sir Richard reflected on this before answering and then he partially evaded the question. 'I suppose like all experienced commanders he had these things in mind, but sometimes I was surprised at his apparent lack of appreciation of the value of good intelligence when making his plans. He, a man of high intelligence, did not seem to read the jig-saw of information at this disposal, even when the pieces had been put toegther, in the same way as I did. Perhaps he was not too well-briefed or he did not attribute the importance to it which it deserved. Normally, not always, but normally one could with the help of a good intelligence staff make a reasonably accurate guess about where to concentrate one's attack upon the enemy without having to mount an expensive assault all along his defensive positions to find a weak point.

'Just look at some of the many ways intelligence was gathered which in the end gave one the precious picture. Our aerial photographs, patrolling, interrogation of prisoners, interception of wireless messages, and even civilians straying between the lines all contributed vital information. We had dozens of sources for the clues we wanted. You will recall from your own experience how we even located the enemy mortars and guns by taking compass bearings on their flashes at night time from different positions, so that by a simple process of triangulation we could work out where they were sited. But that is all self evident. It's the interpretation and use of the evidence which is important. To do that one has to have an awareness of the enemy. One has to ask oneself constantly what is he in the habit of doing? This thing "habit" is very important because it enabled me in the final battle for the River Po to predict largely how he would react to certain of my moves. Equally his knowledge of our habit enabled me to lull him into the conviction that he could predict ours when in fact I was planning something spectacularly different. Hence that vital element of surprise which I mentioned earlier. I know I shouldn't say it but that battle was a magnificent feat of arms.'

'Looking back on it,' I asked him, 'how do you now see it all and what were your crunch problems?'

He carefully weighed this question and settled down to what I knew was going to be a long and considered answer. I edged myself into a more comfortable position so that I could take notes discreetly.

'It really was a nightmare that winter of 1944–45, because not only had the Eighth Army been fighting almost continuously since landing in Italy but the toll of those innumerable river crossings all the way up could not only be measured in the many thousands of casualties and severe loss of equipment and supplies but also in the numbing battle weariness of those who were left.

'You will recall that when we broke through via Rimini into the edge of the Po valley we had virtually shot our bolt. We were strung out right across Italy on a wafer-thin line. We were starved of supplies. At a time when the enemy were sending in fresh divisions to face us, so that they outnumbered us I had to find thousands of troops to send over to Greece to help sort out the nonsense in Athens.' (He was referring to the fighting which broke out there between factions of Greek partisans when the Germans started withdrawing and it looked as if Greece having being rid of the common enemy could fall to a Communist coup).

'It really was a ridiculous situation. Not only were we battle-weary, depleted, depressed, out-numbered and generally mucked about but we who could least afford to find manpower were being asked to send whole formations to France and to Greece, and at a time, I may add, when we were being ordered simultaneously to nail down sufficient divisions of the enemy to make a worthwhile contribution to the whole war effort. It was like being asked to pull a rabbit out of the hat when one found that the rabbit had disappeared and then to one's horror one found that one had been deprived of the hat as well.

'Fortunately, Alexander, Mark Clark, Truscott and I were united in our purpose of achieving a total victory in Italy. Our reasons may not have been quite the same in all respects but in that aim we were completely united. Frankly, Alexander was the man who helped us all to put it together. Surrounded by the broken pieces of his previous efforts when he had been thwarted and let down by people and events, he gathered everything up. It was he with Churchill who saw the importance of going through the Balkans and getting a territorial advantage in Europe for the Allies before the Russians got there. We were one hundred per cent with him and we could have made it by using the beaches in Yugoslavia, beaches which Tito would have protected for us. Can you imagine the luxury of going through a beach-head which was neither an Anzio nor a Salerno but one which was already secure? It was he who deployed such tact, skill and devastating argument who persuaded Alanbrooke and the powers that be in Whitehall that Italy was no longer to be written off as a very minor theatre of war with no prospects. Not only that, he got their support to have new supplies and weapons sent to us when they could have been excused for thinking that we were mad, quite mad, for taking any initiative at all. I suppose indeed we were all mad. I for one was keen that the Eighth Army should end its long march on the same positive note as the one on which it started at Alamein. I knew in my bones that although we were outnumbered, and at times, let me confess, out-manoeuvred by Kesselring's forces we had it in us to strike one quick decisive blow which would probably be less expensive in lives than taking it lying down and watching our casualties pile up by attrition. Truscott was spoiling for a fight. He was great. Very professional. Very frank and forthright. No "ifs" or "buts" as far as he was concerned. Given half a chance he would always be audacious. Mark Clark, on the other hand, I suspect must have savoured the situation because a decisive final victory would make him the Man of Destiny I somehow imagined he always wanted to be, and in fairness I should add not without justification.

'But during all this agonising period we had some things going for us. We had aerial supremacy. The support we had there was derived from the Desert Air Force which I believe to be the most skilled tactical air power in the world. It was the key to our survival and to our attack.

'I had General Freyberg. He and his fine New Zealand divisions gave us backbone. He was a great fighter who not only had to take the brunt of battle but had to do so conscious of his responsibility in not wasting the lives of his men who embodied a whole nation. He was probably the only commander who had a private line to his Cabinet!

'I had General Anders, who in some ways was the greatest of all. He and his Polish Corps who marched out of Russia, through the Middle East, and arrived in time to capture Cassino were an incredible lot. He gave me my biggest shock and my biggest inspiration.'

General McCreery sat back and contemplated me for a few seconds before telling me about the shock he referred to, and which will be described later. He then continued: 'This was one of the crunch problems you asked me to tell you about but at the end I think they only had two problems. One was Mark Clark, the other was how to get an army over a river which was so narrow in places that even a one-legged man could jump it.' I raised my eyebrows in surprise. Surely by this time Mark Clark could not be a problem and as for the river surely he could not be referring to the mighty Po! His eyes creased slightly into a smile.

'Let us deal with the river first,' he said. 'You will remember that before our big battle started we were lined up for weeks beforehand behind the flood banks of the Senio. That was the river fairly wide in parts and very narrow in parts. As I said, so narrow in parts that it could be jumped. But those floodbanks, they were a problem. They were in places very high and wide enough to take 3-ton trucks. The Germans on their side made them impregnable. They had sited magnificent machine-gun posts which had been tunnelled from every angle. Every inch was covered with booby traps, trip wires, and every inch where a soldier might put his foot was mined as well. They had constructed interlocking observation posts, sound detection apparatus, flares for night time illuminations. They had large comfortable bomb-proof dug-outs where reserves could be held to be switched in safety and unseen behind their floodbank wall to any given point. Some dug-outs were even sound-proofed so that they could all have a good sleep when off-duty. We had difficulty in getting a two man patrol across under cover of darkness without being detected.

'How was I to get an army across with sufficient element of surprise to give them a fighting chance before they were shot to pieces? This was a problem which had to be solved and solve it we did.

'As regards Mark Clark, I had a continuous problem with him. Not that we did not get on well together, but I had to be on my guard the whole time to prevent him giving orders or misinterpreting events which would inadvertently undermine Alexander's expressed objectives and overall strategy. Mark Clark felt a little sorry for me, I think. Although he gloried in the fact that, as he put it, he had been entrusted with Britain's "precious Eighth Army" he really thought the Eighth

Army had had it. He felt it was not only worn out but had not the will to fight any more. Consequently he saw the Fifth Army and his own American element as the prime force when it came to combat and they would get the glory while the Eighth Army was consigned to a secondary role. In the event Alexander, Truscott and I and the superb Chief of Staff at Mark Clark's HQ obtained the consensus on planning and battle orders which ensured that everybody played their part according to sensible considerations and not prejudices. It did not matter that as a result Mark Clark would get the glory so long as we won.'

At this point we discussed the enigma of Mark Clark and I told him of my conversation with Alexander which took place in a stable in Benevento. As previously recounted General McCreery expressed the opinion that Alexander was 'livid' about Mark Clark's attitude in going for Rome before giving the coup-de-grace to the retreat of the German Tenth Army.

'But you know,' he continued, 'we all had problems in understanding each other. Think of the extraordinary number of nationalities involved in Italy. Even at the end I was faced with having a Jewish Brigade under my command and while I am sure they were all fine soldiers I could not help but feel that every time I committed them to action they were not so intent on beating the Germans as learning all the lessons they could to continue the war against us in Palestine!

'I had several Italian divisions at my bidding but I could not give them a job in a main attack. They had little equipment and even less will to fight. In fact there was one Italian General who looked so dour and unhappy, I can't remember his name, that I gave orders for him to be excluded from conferences and my 'Order Group' sessions because he so depressed everybody!

'I had Greek troops who were doughty fighters, never lacked courage, but who were apt to go off and do their own thing and forget whose side they were meant to be on. You can imagine, incidentally, what a problem we all had at every level in trying to make ourselves understood with so many different languages to contend with. It was one thing to have the services of interpreters in the fairly civilised and unhurried atmosphere of the planning sessions in my General Headquarters but how could one expect Polish soldiers to explain in their native language to a British tank crew that unless they opened fire immediately on the farmhouse ahead they would be knocked off by a German anti-tank gun? So we went into intensive training with all the different nationalities co-operating together in basic tactical exercises and we devised a simple sign language especially for the tank crews and the infantry to be able to communicate with each other. Sounds obvious but it took some doing. Let us see how many different nations and ethnic groups we had fighting as allies in Italy.'

He paused and then started to list them. At intervals I would come in with my own recollection and together with compiled this astonishing list of no less than thirty-two elements all having identifiable racial characteristics.

There were the Americans. They included a complete negro division and also one of American-Japanese who must have been as confusing to the enemy as they were to us. The British were represented by half a million men and women drawn from every corner of the British Isles, England, Ireland, Scotland and Wales. There were the Canadians including the French from Quebec. Then there were those from New Zealand, South Africa and Newfoundland. There were large Polish, Indian, French, Singhalese and Italian contingents. Others represented were Basuto, Bechuana, Brazilian, Swazi, Seychelles, Rodriquez, Caribbean, Cypriot, Greek, Syro-Lebanese, Jewish, Yugoslav, Nepalese, Belgian and Goumiers from North Africa.

'In all this hotch poch,' I asked him, 'how did the British soldier strike you?'

'I believe him to be the meat in the stew,' he replied. 'Not only was he the most solid part but the most readily identifiable. But one had to remember that basically the British soldier does not consciously fight for his king and country as we sometimes like to think. He only fights for his regiment and he will fight like hell if his regiment is a good show. If it is not a good show he will go under. Good regiments only make good armies because they provide a good soldier. It is all so simple, and I hate to think of regiments losing their identities through amalgamations and the like for the sake of economy, because something which it has taken hundreds of years to build is utterly destroyed. It is the sort of vandalism which only the "quill driving" scribblers in Whitehall, as Wellington once described them, could devise.'

So we chatted on and towards the end of our meeting we discussed the terrific war of movement we were able to maintain by night as well as day during the advance on the Po. This had been greatly assisted by the creation of 'artificial moonlight' as it was called. Searchlight units previously used to protect ports and other installations from enemy aircraft sorties were brought forward to but a few miles behind the front line. When darkness came they switched on and the reflection of their beams suffused the whole of the countryside with a dim light which enabled tanks and convoy movements to be accelerated.

To the enemy in a static defence position it was not all that helpful, especially as he never knew as we did when and where the searchlights would be switched off. But to the attacker it was a godsend because he could maintain his presence and initiative which otherwise in total darkness would have been halted. This innovation came comparatively late in the Italian Campaign and drew from Sir Richard the following observation which from an experienced general of his calibre and armoured warfare expert at that must surely be gospel. He said :

'I have always been of the opinion that if General Montgomery had used his armour more decisively at El Alamein the scale of the victory would have been far more impressive. But this I can tell you. I am one hundred per cent certain that if we had had the wit to use artificial moonlight at El Alamein in conjunction with just one armoured brigade, so that the tanks could go hell bent for their objective, not only would we have won the battle a day earlier, and think of what that would have meant in terms of saving lives, but Rommel would have been written off altogther. Yes, I repeat. He would have been written off completely.'

It was well after eight o'clock when he courteously escorted me to the entrance to the Club and we said goodbye. He died nearly three years later on 18th October 1967, and I wondered how it was that fate conspired to produce a splendid obituary notice in the *Daily Telegraph* the next day which had as its companion in the same page the large picture of General Mark Clark smiling down at a happy laughing woman. The caption read :

General Mark Clark, 71, Commander of the United States Fifth Army in the 1939–45 war, standing with his bride, Mrs Applegate, after a private wedding ceremony at the General's home in Charleston, South Carolina. General Clark's first wife and Mrs Applegate's first husband both died last year.

It seemed as if the entwining of their battle tested and sometimes brittle relationship could only produce such a coincidence.

10.   General Wladyslaw Anders

'The best generals in any theatre of the war
on both sides fought it out to the finish
when we fought for the Po.'

GENERAL ANDERS

It is a curious fact that when Britain was standing alone against Hitler
in the earlier years of the war, when Alexander was engaged in salvag-
ing the British Expeditionary Force at Dunkirk, while Mark Clark and
McCreery were in limbo awaiting the events which ultimately would
set them on their separate ways to link up in North Africa, there was in
1940 a remarkable man languishing in solitary confinement in the
infamous Lubljanka prison in Moscow. This man would one day meet
up with them all to play a decisive part in the war. He suffered torture
and degradation by the Russians of the most cruel nature for twenty
months. He was then fifty years of age. His body bore the scars of no
less than eight wounds. One would hardly believe that not only would
he survive but he would get out of Russia at the head of an army a
hundred thousand strong. He would then march that army through
Iran, Iraq, Syria, the Middle East, North Africa and arrive in time to
capture Cassino. He would then go on to play a key role in the final
triumph in the battle for the River Po.

He was General Wladyslaw Anders, a Russian by birth who in deed
and spirit was a great Polish patriot. A simple recital of the facts will
leave nobody in any doubt that his story is quite astounding. He was
born in 1892 in Lithuania, which was then a Catholic province. So
although he was a Pole by descent he was technically a Russian subject
and his father was actually a high official in the Tsarist government.

After studying mechanical engineering at Riga, he entered the
Russian Army and had risen to the command of a cavalry squadron

by the time the Russian forces were fighting the Germans in World War I. He was wounded five times.

In 1918 he returned to Poland and was a prominent agitator for the re-establishment of Polish independence. He took command of a Polish cavalry squadron when the Polish-Bolshevik war broke out in 1919 and conducted a brilliant campaign against the Russians as the war dragged on through 1920.

When Germany invaded Poland in 1939 General Anders commanded a Polish cavalry brigade. So once again he was fighting the Germans with horses against their tanks. Nearly trapped in East Prussia, he was wounded once more in fighting his way out, only to find that now the Russians were invading Poland. So he turned upon the Soviet troops entering from the east and received his seventh and eighth wounds as his brigade was attempting to cross into Hungary. Finally he was captured by the Russians and with hundreds of thousands of other Poles, many of whom died of the hardships imposed by the Russians, in some instances they were massacred in cold blood, he was held in isolation.

Although he considered himself naturally to be an honourable prisoner of war he suffered great humiliation and indignities, so one can imagine his shock and astonishment when one day in August 1941, the door of his prison cell was opened and Beria, the notorious and dreaded chief of Russia's secret police, entered and gave him a smart salute. He informed General Anders that as the Germans had invaded Russia he was now to be their honoured guest and ally. The Poles were to be invited to fight for and not against their captors. If ever the cliché 'a turn up for the book' meant anything, this was it.

Still recovering from his wounds received in action against both the Germans and the Russians, he was vacated from his cell and driven immediately to a nice apartment, given many comforts including clean linen, and had no less than three servants to wait upon him. He spoke Russian fluently and within a matter of hours despite a hard-hitting conversation with Stalin about the treatment of the Polish prisoners he found himself appointed Commander-in-Chief of the Polish forces in Russia. Stalin even went so far as to mark his esteem by presenting General Anders with a personal present. This was a solid gold cigarette case studded with a magnificent diamond.

It is a matter of history and of one of the most remarkable stories of endurance and heroism how General Anders seized the opportunity to extricate so many of his beloved Poles from Russia. Fired in equal parts by his desire to get them away from their appalling forced labour camps and his passion to use them as the spearhead to win back independence one day for Poland, he was more a Messiah working a miracle than a soldier mobilising an army.

On 14 September 1941 he paid his first visit to a camp where some of his countrymen had been released to form an infantry division. His own description of this event in his book *An Army in Exile*[1] needs no embellishment in setting out the problem and the spirit which enabled it to be conquered.

There for the first time I saw 17,000 soldiers paraded for my arrival. I shall not forget the sight as long as I live, nor the mingled pity and pride with which I reviewed them. Most of them had no boots or shirts, and all were in rags, often the tattered relics of old Polish uniforms. There was not a man who was not an emaciated skeleton and most of them were covered with ulcers, resulting from semi-starvation, but to the great astonishment of the Russians, including General Zhukov, who accompanied me, they were all well shaved and showed a fine soldierly bearing. I asked myself whether I could ever make an army of them, and whether they could ever stand the strain of a campaign. But I found an immediate answer : it was sufficient to note their shining eyes, to see the strong will and faith there. I passed slowly along the front line, we looked enquiringly into one another's eyes, and the first ties were formed for the soldierly journey we had to undertake together. Old soldiers cried like children during Mass, the first they had attended for so many months, and when the hymn 'Our free country give us back, O Lord' was sung, it seemed as if the surrounding forest echoed a hundredfold answer. For the first time in my life, and I hope the last, I took the salute of a march past of soldiers without boots. They had insisted upon it. They wanted to show the Bolsheviks that even in their bare feet, and ill and wounded as many of them were, they could bear themselves like soldiers on their first march towards Poland.

There was no doubt that General Anders commanded the devotion and respect of his soldiers in a manner which was awesome to behold. The first time I was aware of his presence I did not even see him. It was at San Michele near Cassino where with the help of an interpreter I was briefing the officers of a Polish machine-gun unit who were going to take over our gun positions near the Monastery. Suddenly one of them whispered something, whereupon as one man they stood up to

[1] Reproduced by kind permission of Mrs Irena Anders.

attention. There, rigid, silent, and all facing a barely discernible track which ran through the olive trees nearly a hundred yards away each held his respectful stance for a good ten seconds before sitting down again.

I began to think, even to congratulate myself, that I must have said something quite impressive to have prompted such a spontaneous reaction when the interpreter apologised for the interruption and explained. The fact was that the one who whispered had spotted General Anders passing by in his jeep and, although he was a long way off and almost certainly could not have seen us, the reflex of his officers paying their tribute was absolutely instantaneous. Even after the war when his army had been demobilised, resulting in many Poles trying to make a new life for themselves in Britain, I had heard of this same attitude being demonstrated in the unlikely environment of a well-known London restaurant. It appears that General Anders, then a civilian and not in uniform, went in to dine. Within seconds the whole place was brought to a standstill as a number of his men now serving as waiters recognised him instantly and insisted on standing to attention and then according him a round of sustained applause.

So it was not without a certain sense of anticipation mixed with apprehension that in one glorious morning in late March 1965 I presented myself at 20 Princes Gate, not far from London's Knightsbridge and facing Hyde Park, to meet the legendary General Anders by prior appointment. I had told him of my conversations with Alexander, Mark Clark and McCreery and had sent him a detailed synopsis of what I was proposing to say about his Polish Army with the request that he might like to comment on this and to check it for accuracy. I was met by an elegant, charming and somewhat aristocratic gentleman who was obviously more than a private secretary to the General. He appeared to be a companion and confidant and acted as our interpreter using faultless English. The General who was an accomplished linguist employed an interpreter, I suspect, not so much because he did not speak nor understand English both of which aspects he must by then have mastered to a considerable degree, but because it gave him time to think and it was a double check on there being no ambiguity nor misunderstanding in the conversation.

He was about six foot high, lean, alert, with a close-clipped moustache and icy blue eyes. He gave me the hint of a re-assuring smile of welcome.

'You are much younger than I thought you would have been,' he said through his interpreter. 'In Poland, France and Italy you were

lucky to get a command in the army of even a battalion before the
age of forty, but in Britain they put in mere boys.' I admitted that
having had seven years service I was still only twenty-seven years of age
when I was demobilised. He was really referring to peacetime conditions when, as in the British Army, promotion was painfully slow.

'I have read your story about the Polish contribution in the final
battle in Italy.' He paused. 'My country's contribution,' he reiterated
as if to remind me that this came from the free independent Poland
for which he never gave up the fight, and not that Poland which
presently bore the stigma of being a satellite of Russia. 'I am grateful
to you for being very fair about it but permit me to say a little bit more
about the events in the early part of 1945, because your readers may
not understand fully why I was prepared, why we the Poles were
prepared, to let down our friends. It was not simply because they had
let us down it was because I could not ask my men any more to sacrifice
their lives when their future, a future for which so many of us had
died in the previous year, had now been sacrified behind our
backs.'

The agony of General Anders was revealed to me in a way that cut
my heart to ribbons. In quiet but clipped tones, without a trace of
bitterness, he sat upright in his chair and told his story. The background
to it was arguably one of the most infamous political acts of all time.
Briefly at what were known as the Big Three conferences at Yalta and
Teheran, it was decided by America, Britain and Russia that on
Germany surrendering the whole of Poland would be dominated by
Russia. Although Churchill who foresaw more clearly than anyone else
the long-term imperialism of the Soviets had tried to secure a more
acceptable solution for the Poles, it was Roosevelt and later Truman
who swung in favour of Stalin and settled the issue. In Anders' opinion
they both sent Poland to its death, with Churchill an unwilling acces-
sory after the fact.

'It is impossible for anyone who is not a free Pole to understand what
this meant to my men. We had marched thousands of miles together.
We had endured great hardships together. We had fought great battles
together and had suffered thousands of casualties. We had come from
the torture of the Russian labour camps to the brink of a battle which
would seal our claim to be allowed to go home. Suddenly we are told,
without ever being consulted, that we have no home to go to. What
had we been fighting for? What was there left to fight for? A man does
not fight to win a battle so that other people can go to their homes
and he not to his. We had given everything we could to help our friends

to win their battles so that we could win our final battle which was simply to have the right to return to a free Poland.

'After much heart searching and consultation with my senior officers I felt compelled to tell General McCreery that I could not ask my men to go on risking their lives for nothing, for nothing, and I informed him formally of our decision to withdraw the Polish Corps from future operations.'

Then General Anders recounted the incident which made the battle for the River Po not only a strange one by any criteria, but probably unique. Here was the Fifteenth Army Group poised for its final offensive and suddenly it was faced with the prospect of a mass walkout by a hundred thousand of its finest fighting men. This was the bombshell which jeopardised the entire operation and which to General McCreery was one of the really 'crunch' problems mentioned in the previous chapter.

'You will understand,' continued General Anders, 'that I had no other choice. I was angry and sick at heart and I had no right to ask my men to follow me any more. They had given me their loyalty and their lives on the simple promise of my bringing them back one day to their homes in a free country. Where was my promise now? When I explained all this to McCreery, he understood. I expected him to argue with me, to try and talk me round by somehow making excuses about the Big Three decisions, to offer me long explanations and lectures about the implications of my proposal. But no he did not do that. He spoke to me as one soldier to another. He told me very quietly that if I took away my Polish Corps I would leave a ten mile gap. Then he asked me to put myself in his position and suggest how this ten mile gap in the Allied front line could be filled. I was shaken by this simple down-to-earth response. All my pent up emotions and anxieties, all the complexities, all the many pressures and arguments and counter-arguments had been reduced by one single sentence to one single physical consideration, the crux of a ten mile gap.'

General Anders paused to allow me to absorb the significance of it all.

'That's a lot of gap,' I said. It was the sort of idiotic and banal remark which one tends to offer when one does not know what to say.

He took a more lenient view. In fact he took it up. 'You are quite right. It is a lot of gap because in trying to seal it you weaken your effort elsewhere and in this case having virtually no reserves McCreery would have to postpone and re-think the Po battle. In the end I knew in my heart what I had to do. If we who were fighting for a free Poland did not fight in this last battle not only might we ruin the Allied victory in Italy but we would forfeit the chance of our continuing to fight for our independence. I went back to my men and the logic of this argument prevailed. If we fought we just still had a chance of influencing events in our favour. To support our friends even though we ourselves had been betrayed gave us even more moral justification for getting the Big Three to listen to us, and to put right the great wrong they had inflicted upon us. I told McCreery that we would fight on.'

As he spoke I reflected with great sadness that in the event not only did this wonderful man fulfil his promise but in so doing he and his gallant Poles suffered even further provocation. When it came their turn to march into battle to storm the key town of Bologna, the air support they had been promised went wrong. The heavy bombers of the US Air Force mistook their targets and their lethal loads hit the Poles causing tremendous casualties.

McCreery told me that when he heard about this he was not only horrified but expected General Anders quite justifiably to say, 'Look, I was hard put to get my men to go into action at all after the way you have treated us but to be bombed by you as well is truly the last straw. This time we *are* pulling out.' But instead the incredible Anders who had given his word said that not only would he continue to attack but when asked if he wanted more air support he said 'Yes, they have made a mistake once they will not do it again.'

As I sat there the tragedy of these exiled Poles hit me anew. I felt quite sick. Because having suffered so much and having endured what they had endured from 1940 onwards, here they were twenty years later still in a foreign country and still no nearer the liberation of their homeland. General Anders possibly sensing my melancholy took up the conversation, 'No matter how bad things are they could be worse. At least we are free. Come now let us talk more about your battle.' Whereupon I asked him a number of wide ranging questions which elicited thoughtful answers, some of them not without their surprises as the following snatches will show.

'I regard the planning of the battle for the River Po as being quite exceptional because by the time we got there, we, I mean General Mark Clark, McCreery, Truscott, and above all Alexander had gone through so many battle phases we were in danger of thinking we knew all the answers. In fact our common experience taught us so many of the same lessons that we were able to spend more time identifying and discussing the nature of the special problems and we came up with the better solutions.

'I tend to share Alexander's view that the German soldier must be regarded as one of the finest in the world. Just look at what we threw at him and somehow he always managed to throw it back.

'I know it has been a source of mystery and sometimes of amusement that despite our casualties we Poles managed to keep up our fighting strength. Among the many prisoners we took in Italy there were always some Poles who had been forced to fight in the German army and who were glad to join us. But they did that of their own free will. It was a matter of pride to me that our Parade State sometimes showed our casualties being exceeded by those recruited in this unusual way.'

(The Parade State was a periodic return one made to higher HQ showing the number of officers and men who were killed, wounded, missing, sick, on leave etc thus determining the final number available for active duty).

'There were marked differences between the Americans and the British and ourselves but there were none when it came down to who could dig the fastest foxhole. Fear and survival gave each man equal shovel power.

'You ask me at what point I felt sure that the battle for the River Po was won. With hindsight I can now say with certainty that it was won in the first ten minutes. The time it took the Eighth Army to cross the Senio. From that and the amazing capture of the Argenta Gap all success was created.'

'The German generals like Kesselring and Von Vietinghoff who fought us in Italy were Germany's best. Their handling of battles was always competent and sometimes masterly. Their resourcefulness in moving their men about and their flexibility in countering our moves produced many stalemates. That is why the River Po battle when their troops actually outnumbered us was such a triumph. This may be an immodest view, but I believe it to be true, the best generals in the war on both sides fought it out to the finish when we fought for the Po.'

Perhaps his most significant and poignant remark I nursed as we shook hands at the door as I left was, 'One of the problems of administration which did not concern us so much as yourselves was letters from home. Our problem was their absence.'

11. 'Why risk your life?'

'Why risk your life at the last minute? . . .
covering the Po you will find a blanket of death . . .
do you remember the hell of the rivers Sangro, Rapido, Liri,
Volturno and Garigliano? . . . Put these rivers all together
and the result will be smaller than PO!'

GERMAN PROPAGANDA LEAFLETS

It was on 12 February 1945, that I received a cryptic message from my commanding officer. It said: 'Prepare to move your Group back to Florence at first light. SF.' We had been in the line in the highest part of the Apennines for one hundred and twenty three days consecutively without relief. This order offered the prospect of paradise at last.

Only one thing puzzled me and that was the 'SF' at the end. It tallied with no initials either personal or otherwise which I could identify. Was it part of a code I should have known? Did it have some hidden and sinister significance? Whatever it was it did not deter us from pulling out with joy to our new civilised rendezvous. In Florence we found clean warm billets and above all we found lovely hot water. The sweat, dirt and grime of months were washed away by the bounty of the bath.

Refreshed and relaxed I tackled my commanding officer a short while afterwards about the meaning of 'SF', which he appeared to have added for some mysterious purpose to what was otherwise a message of the greatest cheer. He burst out laughing. 'It stands for "sparrow fart", you fool,' he said. 'I was merely emphasising that when I said "first light" I really meant dawn chorus time when it is well known by everyone except you that sparrows signal the imminence of dawn by blowing the birds off their perch with a bloody good fart.' I was very chastened. It was quite clear that my army education was still very much in the primary stage.

From Florence we moved with the whole of the 78th Division on to the Eighth Army front near Cesena. This was a town of considerable size some fifteen miles from the perimeter of our bulge in the fiercely contested Po plain. For the first time for months all of us who wore the famous battle-axe sign of our division were together in a peaceful area. But it was by no means restful. In the short breathing space before we went up into the line again we cleaned everything we could lay our hands on from howitzers down to single bullets, from bivouacs to boots, from tarpaulins to trucks, and especially one's personal clothing right down literally to individual bootlaces. It is curious the sense of communal well-being which is derived from thousands of soldiers working together to smarten themselves up.

Then came a spate of inspections. As previously explained, everything a soldier has including his natural endowments and appendages has to be inspected whenever feasible and on occasions even when it was not feasible. The most awesome ordeal was the official visit of the major-general commanding the division. All the kits of the men, company by company, were laid out in flawless uniformity. This degree of orderliness was only achieved by each individual working for hours to fold blankets and socks and shirts in exact alignment with those of his perspiring colleagues next door. Even the humble knife, fork and spoon had to be positioned with slide rule precision within the common pattern. The webbing of one's belt and crossbraces and gaiters were washed, dried out, and then blancoed to conform to the right degree of khaki. All the vehicles of the battalion were lined up perfectly in long rows. There they stood mudguard to mudguard, all clean and oiled, and with their drivers standing stiffly to attention at each side ready to galvanise them with a reassuring roar followed by idle purring at the flick of a sparkling ignition key. Even the dust between the treads of the tyres was washed away or removed with the efficiency of a toothpick by using an oily rag wrapped around a screwdriver. Once the soldiers succumbed to inspection fever there was no limit to the lengths they would go to achieve smartness nor to their ingenuity in achieving it.

One of the problems my Group had was to hide the excess of clothing, weapons and other stores which we had scrounged or picked up inadvertently during the campaign. Any of the stuff surplus to our 'G.1098' requirements – this being the army form setting out maximum entitlement – was automatically confiscated if it came to light during an important inspection. On one occasion at this time the sleuths of an Inspectorate Board were sent along specifically to establish the extent of our booty, so as to deprive us of it. It was regarded as a real challenge by my beloved Cockneys. They were not going to allow anything they had properly acquired by the normal fortunes of war, whether it be something which fell off the back of the proverbial lorry or by the simple process of indenting for a little more than was strictly necessary from the main RASC dumps, to be forfeited without a fight. They won hands down.

The Inspectorate passed here and there an isolated 'German grave' complete with little wooden cross and helmet. Bits of land marked 'Foul Ground', or roped off with the menacing notice 'Beware-Mines' were also carefully avoided. Only the privileged minority knew that in such 'graves' and other areas was buried our treasure. One storeman had dug so many little caches that he had to compile a comprehensive chart showing landmarks, distances, and compass bearings, so that there was no fear of our being overlooked when the 'all clear' was sounded and excavation could commence.

But as those March days in 1945 started to warm, sterner realities had to be faced. The build up for what we all knew in our hearts would be our final and most frightening confrontation with the enemy was under way. Expeditions were sent back into the mountains to dig out and retrieve every box of small arms' ammunition, and case of bombs, of shells, of grenades, and weapons and stores of every kind which had been lost or thrown off mule trains in the nightmare journeys of the past. It was obvious that unless this was done the ration of armaments for the Italian sector, now the forgotten arena of Europe, would be far too meagre to allow our High Command to fulfil their plans, whatever they might be.

At the same time all formations went into arduous battle training. Platoons, companies, battalions, brigades, practised their complicated manoeuvres with supporting artillery and tank units. The emphasis was placed on river crossings which took place in the half light of dusk or dawn. Exceptional attention was given to the speedy deployment of portable pontoons and small boats. The 'sappers' worked against the clock to beat their records in erecting Bailey bridges in a variety of awkward locations designed to test their organisation to the utmost. The familiar pattern of activity before a major offensive was re-enacted in all its other phases, but this time it was different. Despite the exhilaration we were all aware that what we had to do next was not just to cross yet another river, but to cross the one that mattered most. It offered the Germans their greatest bastion of defence. It offered us our greatest grave. It was the River Po. In the years that have passed I have not met a survivor who did not admit that he shared the same deep albeit unspoken sense of apprehension as I did.

The Germans were fully alive to the psychological advantage they enjoyed by having the River Po at their back. Their propaganda leaflets dropped in profusion over our lines got quickly to the point. I will give them here in detail because they will demonstrate how well they appreciated our vulnerability to the sickening horror of the river crossings, and how, having got it right, they spoilt it all by a certain naive presentation which made their exercise largely counter-productive.

Their most graphic leaflet showed on one side British soldiers being blown to pieces midstream as shell bursts capsized their assault boats. Men were drowning in the water made turbulent by the fury of the German gunfire. On the other side we, the intended victims read :

ONE MORE RIVER

But it isn't only 'one more river' – this time
it is THE RIVER !
It is the mighty Po !
Do you remember the hell of the rivers Sangro,
Rapido, Liri, Volturno and Garigliano?
Do you remember the lives that were sacrificed
in crossing these rivers?
Put these rivers all together and the result
will be smaller than the
PO !
Also when you crossed these rivers, the Germans
were in retreat and had no time to prepare defenses.
But covering the Po you will find a blanket of death
. . . artillery, Nebelwerfers, Mortars and Spandaus.
The whole Po area is a network of canals and is
impassable for tanks.
Rush
In !
Various
Exiting
Revelations
Prepared.
Oh Boy !
And here are a few facts about the Po :
At its shallowest part (between Adda and Minicio)
it is 7 ft deep.
At the deepest part (near Pavia) it is 20 ft deep.
The width varies from 208 to 1,040 yds.

The banks are mostly sheer and between 18 and 30 ft.
high.
The speed of the Po exceeds 20 mph.
'PO' means death and suffering.
POW means security and comfort!
Think it over, only
Fools rush in . . . !

It is curious that they tried to dramatise their message by making a
sentence the initial letter of which spelled out RIVER PO when read
vertically and that in the middle of it they should put 'exiting' instead
of 'exciting'. Come to think of it, their intended use of the word
'exciting' in this context was hardly appropriate. It gave one almost
a sense of happy expectation.

A multitude of smaller leaflets hit us at the same time when once
again a somewhat laboured pun in each case rather cancelled any
impact they had. One illustrated a clock with the hands showing five
minutes to midnight. It bore the simple question 'Why RISK your life
in the LAST minute?' On the other side it said 'Don't jump ahead and
lose your head!' Another leaflet had the same wording with the clock
illustration but on the reverse it said 'One who holds back has *more*
chance of holding on!'

Another variant of their propaganda ascribed to the British quite
erroneously a political awareness of the changes brought about by the
death of Roosevelt and the consternation this should have caused us.
On one side was a crude drawing of Stalin sitting both on his chair and
that of Truman. He is smiling benignly at a diminutive Churchill who
is seen scowling in the third seat. On the reverse of the leaflets was a
message headed 'Churchill – without Roosevelt'. I give it here in full
because one can see how this convoluted but not illogical argument
must have been thought up by Dr Goebbels in the expectation that it
would strike dread in the minds of the victims, but Dr Goebbels
boobed. The British were as insensitive, apathetic, and unimpressed
then about global politics as they are to-day. No pieces of paper found
their way more quickly into the latrines than did those with this
message :

The Big Three are now only Two. One has gone . . . His place in
the White House has been taken by the honourable Senator Truman,
who naturally will take Roosevelt's seat on the Council of the Big
Three. And yet – will it be the same ?

Are not the Big Three Churchill, Stalin and – Roosevelt? They are the men that count. These Big Three, who jointly made the plans for the Allied policy and warfare, whose hands held all the reins and on whose personal mutual understanding the cooperation of the Allies depended far more than on treaties or the exchange of views of military leaders and Government officials. However great the weight of the powerful and rich USA may be – in the Council of the Big Three it makes a great difference whether Stalin faces Roosevelt or whether he sits down at the conference table with an obscure senator, who has no experience in international politics and who, up to the present, has only had the title of 'Vice-President' printed on his card.

So Churchill is now alone with his powerful and insatiable ally Stalin – without the weighty word of his friend Roosevelt.

Harry Truman will sit on the third chair. But still – considering the personages he is dealing with – this place is as good as empty.

And Stalin has proved to be a man who sees the chance and grabs it.

On 11th March 1945 we moved forward to take up our medium machine-gun and heavy mortar positions in the front line which was marked literally in three dimensions of awesome magnitude by the flood-banks of the River Senio. I had never seen anything so big like this before. Each flood-bank, built up over the centuries to contain the floodwater from the thawing snows of the northern Apennines, was as high as three London double-decker buses standing on top of each other. Each was wide enough at its summit to permit two double decker buses to pass each other with room to spare.

We held the southern flood-bank except for a few stretches where the enemy held grimly on to outpost positions. This coupled with the fact that the river itself was in places only about thirty feet wide produced a proximity rarely achieved between opposing forces. Consequently there were always brisk exchanges of small-arms fire going on punctuated by marathon hand grenade duels. The activity reached a crescendo when darkness came. It was then that the Germans scattered their machine gun fire like lethal confetti all over our area laced with gigantic 'stonks' from his mortars and Nebelwerfers.

The Senio sector was heavily wooded by the ubiquitous olive and other trees all interconnected by an absolute maze of vines, narrow tracks, and dykes. Hidden at frequent intervals among this patchwork were small farmhouses and outbuildings which afforded excellent billets.

Visibility in any direction was restricted even in daytime by this congestion to less than two hundred yards and all our machine-gun counter harassing fire had to be done indirectly using calculations from our excellent maps.

These showed however a broader picture of the terrain which did little to allay our apprehension about the outcome of the battle for the River Po. In fact we were shaken. We could plainly see that before we even got to the River Po we had five major rivers to cross, repeat five, and all equally well defended by the massive flood-bank ramparts coupled with the skilfully prepared enemy positions at all the vital points. These rivers, the Senio, the Santerno, the Sillaro, the Idice, and the Reno derived their sources in that order several miles apart from the northern Apennines on our left. They flowed northwards towards the Po but then turned right, due east to the Adriatic, to link up with the Reno in a line parallel with the Po itself. It was as if the Po, conscious of the forthcoming battle, had taken the precaution of establishing a multi-pronged deterrent in defence of any violation of its banks.

However, there was an Achilles heel. Two of the rivers, the Sillaro and the Idice, joined up with the Reno near the town of Argenta, on our extreme right. Argenta provided a dry gap between the flooded defence positions which the Germans had created to the south by opening up some flood-banks and the naturally wet marshes linking Argenta with Lake Commachio to the north. If one could capture Argenta then at one blow three rivers would be outflanked, the hinge of the German defensive system would be destroyed, and the way to the Po would be open.

General McCreery used to go up in his 'spotting' plane, a little Lysander, and see Argenta in the distance with the gleaming and mocking waters of the flooded country all round it. 'I used to ask myself,' he told me, 'how can it be done? How can we take Argenta? I only knew that we had to do it somehow. The Eighth Army had fought a lot of battles. It was tired. Mark Clark had rather written us off I think. I knew we could do it and we had to do it, but how?'

The answer was forthcoming in dramatic fashion but in order to understand it one has to appreciate that it only arrived because a number of major problems were first solved successfully.

It was apparent that in the face of such obstacles our normal transport and equipment which was now virtually obsolete would put us at a tremendous disadvantage.

Then glory be, some substantial crumbs from the rich man's table

8th Army troops attacking along the flooded terrain near Lake Comacchio 10th April 1945. Their essential equipment included bandoliers of ammunition and spades for digging in. Steel helmets had nets to carry pieces of artificial or natural camouflage.

A tough brave German paratrooper who died defending his position on the Torrente Idice, the last river line before the River Po and the defence of which the Germans had been working on for a whole year, using forced Italian labour. It was stormed and crossed by the New Zealand troops – Alexander's *Corps de Chasse*.

British soldiers examining examples of the blood-curdling propaganda put over by the Germans. On one side (*above*) a beautiful beckoning girl holding a basket of fruit is captioned 'The Po is waiting for you.' On the other side (*below*) the figure 'Death' is seen rising from the River Po with British dead all around.

Men of 5 Northants 78th Division in the badly battered town of Argenta. Note the appalling rubble and debris over which the hard fighting took place. Tanks could not get through.

Crossing of the River Po, 25th April 1945 – transport destroyed by air attack.

(*Left*) A symbolic picture of the River Po. A British soldier reflects on what a battle for its possession might have meant while gazing on its wide but peaceful waters.

(*Below*) New Zealand sappers commence work on a floating pontoon bridge across the River Po, 25th April 1945.

turned up. Released or diverted from the Western Front came flame-throwing tanks, special troop carrying tanks, amphibious tanks, and tanks that carried their own bridges for river crossings. This exciting equipment required new tactics to be worked out and the development of teamwork between infantry, tank crews and the air-force whose fighter bombers would give close support. Co-operation was vital. It had to be rehearsed over and over again. The Fifteenth Army Group was drawn from so many different parts of the world that a situation could and did arise where attacks were made with the infantry, tank crews and gunners involved all speaking impossibly different languages ranging from Polish to Hindi. The exchange of interpreters, the development of a simple sign language and above all the mutual respect and trust born of the comradeship of arms and of perils shared enabled the strangely assorted races to communicate in double quick time.

During this period the four commanders, Alexander, Clark, McCreery and Truscott, were talking through their plans. They were all agreed on Alexander's firmly stated objective namely that the German Army Group 'C' must be destroyed south of the Po. But they were not all agreed about the method. Both McCreery and Truscott had tremendous arguments with Mark Clark. The latter wanted Truscott's Fifth Army to make the main offensive on a line converging from the right on to Bologna, whereas Truscott wished to do it on a line more to the left. Mark Clark told McCreery that the Fifth Army would be responsible for the major attack and the Eighth Army while doing their best to contain the enemy on their Senio front should have no more than a supporting role.

McCreery was nettled. 'I spoke to Alexander about it,' he told me. 'I felt justified in going behind Mark Clark's back because the whole thing was such a hash and I was confident the Eighth Army could play just as an important part in the operations especially as at that time we had more divisions to deploy than the Americans. If I had mentioned to Mark Clark my intention to question his orders with Alexander, as I would normally have done as he was my immediate superior, I knew Mark Clark would create hell. It would embarrass Alexander and spoil the very real respect and understanding we all had for each other. In the event, and I cannot say to what extent Alexander had a hand behind the scenes, both Truscott and I did it our way while conforming sufficiently to Mark Clark's plan to avoid any direct conflict with his directive. It was not a question of a conspiracy. In fact it was because Mark Clark was posing problems for all of us that he sharpened our awareness of what we had to do and of our assessment of all the factors. As far as I was concerned I made my plans following my talks with Alexander on the simple premise that the Eighth Army would make just as an important contribution if not better than that envisaged by Mark Clark for Truscott.'

The plan which ultimately emerged was not the 'broad front' foray which characterised so many of Mark Clark's previous battles. It was the classic one-two punch which was the hallmark of so many desert battles and of General Montgomery's tactic in the weeks following the D-Day landings in Normandy. One delivered a blow on one flank of sufficient pressure and magnitude to draw the enemy's reserves and then at the 'moment critique' one brought over a left or right hook for the knock-out. But here in Italy it was as absurdly simple on paper as it was diabolically difficult to put into effect on the ground.

The Eighth Army in the low-lying land on the Adriatic side was to launch an all-out attack on 10th April (later advanced to 9th April) and having crossed a number of river obstacles to chase due north like a scalded cat and cross the River Po before the enemy could organise his defences there. This would have the effect of engaging the enemy's enthusiastic attention and drawing his reserves away from the US Fifth Army front. The latter would then fight their way out of the mountains a few days later and having captured the key central town of Bologna on the edge of the Po plain, would dash due north too and cross the Po as quickly as possible.

During the weeks preceding the attack General Mark Clark visited his troops along the whole front using a tiny plane – which he called affectionately 'my cub'. He must have pondered long and hard about the complexity of his armies. There were so many different races represented with different skins, religions, languages, customs, appetites and attitudes.

On the Eighth Army front troops from the United Kingdom predominated. There were the great London regiments like the Royal Fusiliers, London Irish, London Scottish, Princess Louise's Kensington Regiment and a host of other units. The famous county regiments were there like the East Surreys, The Buffs, the Queen's Royal Regiment (West Surrey), the Queen's Own Royal West Kent, Lancashire Fusiliers, the Northamptonshire Regiment, the Middlesex, the Cheshires and the Durham Light Infantry.

There were the proud Scottish names – the Argyll and Sutherland Highlanders, the Lovat Scouts, Highland Light Infantry, Lothians and Border Horse and others. From Wales came the Welsh Regiment and

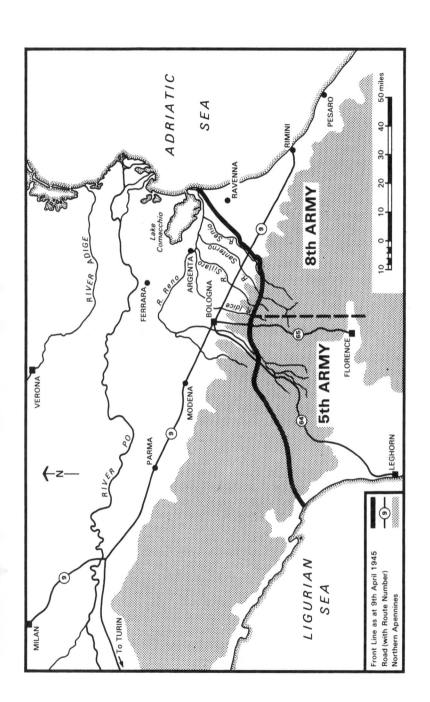

ADRIATIC SEA

PESARO

RIMINI

RAVENNA

8th ARMY

9

Lake Comacchio

R. Senio

R. Santerno

R. Sillaro

ARGENTA

R. Reno

(Idice)

BOLOGNA

FERRARA

65

RIVER ADIGE

5th ARMY

FLORENCE

MODENA

9

64

PARMA

RIVER PO

VERONA

LEGHORN

N

MILAN

9

To TURIN

RIVER

9

LIGURIAN SEA

Northern Apennines

Road (with Route Number) 9

Front Line as at 9th April 1945

50 miles
40
30
20
10
0
10

Welsh 'Gunner' Regiments. The Welsh Guards were there too, with the other constituent battalions of the immortal Guards Brigade.

The Irish turned up in force. Not only were there battalions of the Royal Inniskilling Fusiliers, Royal Irish Fusiliers and the London Irish Rifles carrying the fighting tradition of the historic Irish Brigade, but there were the North Irish Horse and thousands of Irishmen from the neutral South who had infiltrated into every unit in the country – all keen to get into the fight while applauding De Valera's astuteness in keeping them 'out of the war'.

There were the great cavalry regiments in the armoured Brigades like the Lancers and Queens Bays, there was the famous 2nd Parachute Brigade, there were Royal Marine and other Commando Units as well as units of the Rifle Brigade and the King's Royal Rifle Corps.

So large and diverse were the forces from the British Isles that there can have been few families from John O'Groats to Lands End who did not have a stake in Italy at this time.

This was also true of New Zealand who had presented the Eighth Army with one of its finest divisions which included a complete battalion of Maoris.

From India came great soldiers from the Punjab, Jaipur, Mahratta and Baluchistan. There were the Sikhs and the Gurkhas – all with their individual problems. Just to illustrate one of the minor ones, a herd of goats had to be maintained behind the lines to provide food for the thousands of Indians whose religion prevented them from eating pork!

There was the entire Polish Corps which as already related was recruited from the brave exiles who had escaped from many parts of Europe after their country had been overcome.

Completing the main forces of the Eighth Army was the Jewish Brigade comprising three Palestine regiments. In addition there were formations of Italians who had been partially equipped and trained by the British but who could not be used as front line shock troops. They did useful work in plugging gaps and routine patrolling.

The Fifth Army also had a fascinating segment of the world's population. There was a preponderance of American GI's drawn from every part of the States but what was interesting was that a complete Negro division was included and also a complete Japanese-American regiment. Then there was the South African Armoured Division with strong Afrikaans speaking elements. Italian units, again trained by the British, were also found in this sector and bringing this motley array to an end there was a whole Brazilian Infantry Division.

The arrival of the Brazilians in the winter had caused a near panic in finding Portuguese-speaking interpreters to say nothing of the complications they added to the supply problem. Not only were they wearing light clothing – all right for Rio de Janeiro but not much good for Apennine blizzards – but in re-equipping them a curious fact emerged. It was found that they had much smaller feet than the average American or British soldier and finding sufficient footwear of the right size became a quartermaster's nightmare.

The Germans too had brought a number of 'volunteers' into their regiments from occupied countries. Poles, Czechs, Hungarians and a sizeable contingent of White Russians had all been identified.

Surely never before were such a variety of nations to become enmeshed in battle. In the final line-up we had seventeen divisions, some armoured brigades and four Italian groups. The Germans had no less than twenty-three divisions all up to strength. They included some of their best in any theatre of war like the 1st and 4th Parachute, a Panzer and several Panzer Grenadier Divisions. 'We were not fighting rubbish,' Alexander said using a typical understatement for emphasis. In addition the Germans had four Italian divisions so that they could deploy twenty-seven divisions over all against the equivalent of about twenty on the Allied side.

In the tense weeks of late February and March 1945, not only did our four generals have to instigate all the complicated planning processes and preparatory operations but they had to survive the shock of the threat of the whole Polish Corps pulling out. When General Anders protested bitterly to McCreery about the betrayal of Poland after the Yalta 'Big Three' Conference and asked for his 100,000 men to be withdrawn and treated as prisoners-of-war, it put a stop to everything. All strategic considerations had to be suspended. It was not until McCreery persuaded Anders that his chance of changing the future geography of Poland was better served by fighting on than not fighting at all, that the situation was restored.

Another shock had to be absorbed almost on the eve of battle. There was always the fear that the enemy could disrupt everything either by making a concerted attack at any point or by quickly retiring to a previously prepared position. We had been reminded of the enemy's ability to precipitate a crisis when late in December, only three months before, they launched a most serious attack down a valley on the Fifth Army front which threatened disaster because it might have led to the capture of Leghorn – a port through which came all the Fifth Army supplies. This attack gained good success initially but thanks to smart intelligence work a division had been moved just in time to seal it off. It took a little time to restore confidence especially when an officer of the Durham Light Infantry peering into a large cavernous hole in the ground, enquired of its occupant – an inexperienced negro officer of the US Army – 'Have you seen any Germans?' The negro rolled his eyes. 'No, Sir' he said emphatically. 'We don't see nobody. We don't bother them and they don't bother us.'

It so happened that one evening early in April what looked like a repetition occurred. For several hours from about 6.00 pm enemy gunfire increased along a sector of the Eighth Army front to such a degree that it seemed certain they were about to launch a major offensive. The whole of the 78 Division area was saturated with an intense barrage. One point alone was pinned down by over four thousand shell and mortar bomb bursts. But the attack did not come in. Why not? Was it to cover a withdrawal? We had to know quickly because all the planning could be upset if we got no answer. Out went the patrols and several prisoners were taken. From them we learnt that this bit of violence known to the Germans under code name 'Leonidas I' had three main aims namely to break up our concentration of troops and supplies; to destroy our gun lines; and to cover their withdrawal. None of these were achieved and the withdrawal of the enemy which would have done so much to thwart our plans was countermanded. It seemed that the German High Command had changed its collective mind at the last moment. Hitler even at this stage when he was about to spend his last days in his bunker in Berlin still exerted his authority. He ordered a standfast instead of this well planned withdrawal, and he was obeyed.

This turned out to be fortuitous for the Fifteenth Army Group. But they needed all the luck they could get. When one thinks about it, it was arguably the war's most calculated piece of impertinence for the annihilation of the German Army Group 'C' to be contemplated at all by our commanders. Here they were rising from the ashes of the sad disarray and sagging spirits of our denuded armies and the obstacles they faced as opposed to the reinforced, well-organised and aggressive armies of the enemy. Take one simple aspect. In the light of modern fire-power it was not considered feasible for an attack against prepared positions to succeed without having a numerical superiority of at least three to one. In Normandy at that time we are told that they counted on having a superiority of more than five to one. It is not surprising therefore that Churchill and everyone else – that is except our four generals – assumed that no successful final attack could be mounted in Italy where if there was any numerical superiority at all – it was enjoyed by the enemy!

However, although we were outnumbered on the ground we enjoyed three great blessings. The first was our overwhelming supremacy in the air. This was the crucial factor. It was almost impossible for a single German reconnaissance plane to get over our lines and observe our preparations (except in areas where it was encouraged to do so!) before being shot out of the skies. The second was a long spell of wonderfully fine weather which kept the many rivers which had to be crossed from being swollen. Lastly at army, corps, divisional, brigade, and battalion level we had time to prepare brilliant plans which were all brought to fruition by imaginative battle-hardened leaders at every level. The stage was set. The opposing armies braced themselves. Everybody knew this was the final act. Indeed at the end of March and in the first week of April the Fifth and Eighth Armies had already made their first moves.

12. 'The Führer expects . . .'

'The Führer expects, now as before, . . . to defend
every inch of the North Italian areas . . . I desire
to point out the serious consequences for all
those . . . who do not carry out the Führer's orders
to the last word' . . .

TELEGRAM FROM JODL TO VIETINGHOFF

It was on 18th March 1945 that Mark Clark called a conference of his
army commanders and staffs to take stock of the operations which had
already been put into effect or were being planned as the preliminary
moves in confusing the enemy. At this conference the battle plans were
also discussed for the co-ordination of the final offensive.

McCreery's philosophy of giving the enemy no rest had been well
and truly carried out not only on his own Eighth Army front but along
that of the Fifth Army as well. The Germans were kept busy in all the
wrong places. In February they got a little nudge from the Fifth Army
along the coastal road on the Mediterranean side which attracted their
29th Panzer Grenadier Division into the line. In March they got very
nervous about their other flank on the Adriatic when they noticed a
lot of very ostentatious activity in the port of Ravenna which suggested
the possibility of the Allies making a landing by sea well behind their
lines. Our naval advisers had said this was impossible but it was hoped
that the enemy's knowledge of amphibious warfare would not drive
them to the same conclusion. German 'spotter' planes were sold
'dummies in the form of false gun positions and supply dumps. German
monitors intercepting wireless messages must have been very impressed
by the increased traffic in the Adriatic sector although what they made
of a remark of a British operator who signed off his transmission with
'three cheers for Lili Marlene' will always be in some doubt.

But what is in no doubt at all is that once again the deception plan succeeded magnificently. Enemy formations were scooting all over the place and in the last week of March one of his only two motorized divisions in reserve was moved back from the centre to near Venice to meet the expected sea invasion. Here was a division using up valuable fuel stocks to get to a place where it could not intervene when the real battle started because to come south again it had to cross four rivers including the Po in the face of air attack.

During the first few days in April enemy disquiet increased even more on the Adriatic side when British Commandos using amphibious tanks (nicknamed 'Fantails') moved over the marshy lakes adjoining the sea and came back with nearly a thousand prisoners. More attacks followed in quick succession in the same area where again the Germans were taken by surprise. It is curious how the small human frailty can influence major events, and it would have astonished them to know that but for the fact that one of their NCO's loved eels this might never have happened. This single minded gourmet in charge of a post close to the waters gave permission to Italian fishermen to go out and catch his slimy delicacy and they took the opportunity to cross all the way to the British lines and hand in first class information about the channels that could be navigated and enemy dispositions.

No sooner had the enemy got really jumpy about the Adriatic than the Fifth Army struck a blow right over on the other side on the Mediterranean. On 5th April, aided by massive supporting fire from the heavy guns of the Royal Navy, the Allied attack made good headway. This again was only a diversion but General Lemelson was sufficiently shaken to reinforce his front by the 90th Panzer Grenadiers Division and a couple of independent battalions, all from reserves.

Mark Clark's account of this phase of the operations to me and that of McCreery both bore the same insight into the enemy's thinking. Mark Clark told me : 'We knew the enemy had developed tremendously strong defensive positions along all those natural river obstacles which stood between us and the Po. He knew that we knew and consequently he was always expecting us to do the obvious which was to make thrusts along the sea edge on either flank supported by amphibious landings. So naturally whenever we made a feint in these areas he was half way to thinking it was the real thing before we even started !'

'I have never known,' said McCreery, 'so many well executed diversionary attacks, both real and simulated, which kept the enemy guessing for so long. He was so preoccupied with what he knew we knew about the formidable nature of his defences that he reacted strongly to anything which he thought we would do sensibly to outflank

them. I do not believe he even considered that I was putting myself in
his shoes, or perhaps I should say jackboots, and acting out on Lake
Comacchio what he had more than half expected. Even then we took
him by surprise. However, I think our real triumph at this time was
that he became so occupied with our various deceptions and initiatives
he forgot the one thing which might have turned the scales against us.
He forgot that the best method of defence is to attack. If he had come
at us over the Senio or down the middle of the Italian front I believe
he could have blown us wide open. He had the troops and the fire-
power to do it and such was the nature of the ground that our fine air
force could have given us little close support.'

On 24th March General Mark Clark issued his Operations Instruction No 4* to his Army Commanders and Staff from his Florence
Headquarters. It confirmed the orders given at their meeting six days
earlier. It is interesting to read the preamble if only because here and
there one senses the American tendency to us multi-syllable words to
emphasise the importance of the occasion when more simple words
would have done.

1.   The offensive directed by this operations instruction should
     result in a major disaster to the enemy, and consequently
     have an important effect on the prompt termination of
     hostilities. If fully successful, it should be of so crushing and
     thorough a nature that it will be the last coordinated offensive
     against German forces which the 15th Army Group will
     make. The attention of all ranks within the 15th Army Group
     should be called to the unprecedented opportunities which
     are provided at this time for dealing a mortal blow to the
     enemy and accelerating the day of victory. It is of vital
     importance that each individual who contributes to the
     offensive shall devote fully his energy and abilities to driving
     the attack home to the enemy wherever he may be found, so
     that the maximum number of German troops will be
     destroyed or captured. To this end it is directed that all
     commanders use every effective means to acquaint thoroughly
     the troops under their command with the opportunities that
     lie before them at this time, and that leadership be active
     throughout the operations to exploit fully every phase of the
     situation as it develops.

* See Appendix B.

The Instruction then went on to set the capture of Verona as the main objective for the Fifteenth Army Group with its two armies carrying out the operation in three separate phases in order to achieve it. In Phase 1 the Eighth Army was required to breach the Senio and Santerno rivers and then turn right to break through the Argenta Gap. At the same time the Fifth Army was to be on twenty-four hours notice from two days after the Eighth Army had made its move with the object of making what Mark Clark describes as 'the main effort of Fifteenth Army Group and attack with the mission of debouching into the Po Valley with a secondary mission of capturing or isolating the city of Bologna'. It is interesting to note that Mark Clark still saw the Fifth Army's part of the operation as the 'main effort' of the Fifteenth Army Group which must have depressed McCreery, especially as in Phase II he was given the subsidiary role of 'seizing and holding key road centers' on the Reno river and near the Po, while the term used for the Fifth Army's effort was to 'exploit with armor and infantry' a manoeuvre to join up with the Eighth Army 'thereby completing the encirclement of enemy forces south of the Po River.' There was no reason why McCreery should not have been asked to 'exploit' but it is clear in tone and concept that Mark Clark in his written Instruction did not want to acknowledge that each Army was contributing equally to the final outcome which in fact they were.

Early in April those of us who sensed something was imminent were not privy to the dramas going on behind the scenes, but confirmation that the hour of action was upon us was heralded by the arrival of the inevitable 'Special Order of the Day'. The one transmitted down the line to all troops from Alexander was not unlike the many others we had received in earlier battles but it did have a certain ring of finality. It said :

Final victory is near. The German Forces are now very groggy and only need one mighty punch to knock them out for good. The moment has now come for us to take the field for the last battle which will end the war in Europe. You know what our comrades in the West and in the East are doing on the battlefields. It is now our turn to play our decisive part. It will not be a walk-over; a mortally wounded beast can still be very dangerous. You must be prepared for a hard and bitter fight; but the end is quite certain – there is not the slightest shadow of doubt about that. You, who have won every battle you have fought, are going to win this last one.

Forward then into battle with confidence, faith and determination to see it through to the end. Godspeed and good luck to you all.

We who were up in the front line could be forgiven for having a little scepticism about the outcome because there was nothing to indicate that the pattern of the many previous river crossings when the enemy escaped to fight another day would not be repeated. Indeed a feeling of deep disquiet affected many of us because this was not just one more river crossing, it was an operation demanding at least half a dozen canal and river crossings before even reaching the mighty Po itself. These were all defended by natural earthworks and the well-practised skills of an industrious and resolute foe. My personal pessimism was attributable mainly to two factors.

The first was that I was now suffering from a condition called 'battle fatigue'. This was a euphemism for being just plain 'bomb happy'. Fortunately I recognised the symptoms in time to keep a grip on myself as far as outward appearances went. But inwardly I was tense, morose, and nervy. Each day as I made my way up to the Senio floodbank, a distance of no more than four hundred yards, in order to visit my detachments and the infantry units they supported, I subjected myself to a self-inflicted torture. I walked stealthily along a well-worn track with head well down and eyes straining to catch the tell-tale traces of where a possible mine might still lurk. I scanned the ground on each side of the path with microscopic intensity to discern every possible hollow or cover where in the event of a bullet, bomb or shell fire I could dive for safety. My ears strained to catch the slightest sound of a gun or mortar going off on the enemy's side so that I could be in extra readiness to anticipate the terrifying split second 'swoosh' of the missile's arrival. My ears in fact must have simulated the rotation of radar saucers so sensitive did they become in the detection of long distance hostility. Whenever they did, and it was quite often even on such a comparatively short journey, I broke out instantly into a sweat. Each time I heard a gun go off, no matter how remote, I asked myself, 'Is this it?'

My pre-occupation with my own personal survival became a mania. It even got so far as to my digging in secret a chain of pathetic little slit trenches for myself at points en route where there was no natural cover readily at hand. One might be excused for thinking that this was a sensible precaution against the unexpected vagaries of enemy harassing fire, but no soldier in his right mind would have had the energy or enthusiasm for such negative hard labour when the odds against it offering any real protection were so enormous.

The other factor which was more academic but none the less obsessive as far as I was concerned was the apparent impossibility of getting over even the very first obstacle, namely the blasted Senio itself. I could not see how it could be done. When I crept up into the lee of those enormous floodbanks I was reminded as we had to talk in whispers of the extraordinary situation of the opposing troops living within a few yards of each other under the shelter of their respective escarpments. We all knew from our many intelligence sources that the Senio, narrow as it was at this time, was near impregnable.

By clever tunnelling and well prepared earthworks the enemy had built up listening and observation posts, rifle pits and machine gun posts which made any attempt to cross the river absolutely suicidal. A mouse could not move without being knocked off. In addition there were thousands of mines everywhere on both sides of the enemy bank and on the ground beyond plus pits, traps, barbed wire trip wires, and just in case of real emergency pre-arranged salvoes from mortars and artillery could be called upon at any time to saturate any section on either or both sides of the river. 'Blimey,' remarked one Tommy after being briefed, 'the only killer Old Jerry left out of this little lot is sauer-bloody-kraut.'

Yet somehow the troops had to get over the Senio sufficiently quickly and in such force as to be able to breach the next river, the Santerno, which was defended on almost identical lines. It was very difficult indeed for any of us who analysed the problem at all to envisage any possible solution which did not involve the wholesale slaughter of our own troops. It had to be done, but how?

The first hint of the answer came on that lovely spring day, 9th April 1945. For the Germans, that morning with its soft breeze and sunshine seemed to augur the usual routine. The same old machine-gun harassing fire broke out intermittently. An occasional shell or mortar bomb exploded in the distance. Now and again a stray bullet or the drone of a plane would intrude. It was a morning to tidy up the dug-out, to hang up the washing if there had been any washing to be hung. It was a lazy comfortable morning when sentries thought of home and felt warm and good to be alive.

For the Eighth Army it was not a morning of usual routine. For overnight and from dawn onwards all the troops on the Senio line were very quietly withdrawn several hundred yards back from the floodbanks.

This silent retreat was made under cover of just about the normal harassing fire. The enemy never knew. There was nothing to suspect. Just at ten minutes to two they got the message. This would be a day to remember – that is if they lived. From that moment until nearly half past three – for just about a hundred minutes – eight hundred and twenty five heavy bombers of the Allied Strategic Air Force dropped 175,000 fragmentation bombs covering the enemy gun areas and places where enemy reserves might form up opposite the points where the Eighth Army would attack.

At the same time a thousand of our medium and fighter-bombers attacked such pre-arranged targets as enemy HQs, individual gun positions, mortars, dumps and anything that was caught moving.

There was a lull for about half an hour and then came the moment the Germans on the Senio had been waiting for – the artillery bombardment. From past experience they expected this to be the prelude to an attack which the scale of the bombing in their rear areas presaged. For forty-two minutes a hail of shells and mortar bombs came down and then suddenly silence. Now surely the attack would come in? But no, for the next ten minutes all that came in was a stream of fighter bombers flying literally only a few feet above the flood banks and attacking targets all along the line. Then the artillery and mortars opened up again for another forty-two minutes and again the fighter bombers did their stuff. This pattern continued yet a third time and a fourth time. The Germans by now knew that as soon as the bombardment stopped there was no point in popping their heads out if they heard the sound of the planes coming in. They risked death by exposing themselves to the bullets and bombs of the fighter-bombers and while the strafing went on no Eighth Army troops could cross the river anyway.

On the fifth occasion just before dusk the bemused Germans heard the bombardment stop and once again the familiar scream of the airplane engines kept them huddled in their holes. But this time the fighter bombers only made a 'dummy' run and in those precious few minutes gained before the truth dawned upon the enemy our infantry had crossed the Senio.

Careful rehearsals for weeks beforehand in forming up and then scaling and descending the flood bank with portable pontoon equipment enabled the New Zealanders and 10th Indian Division to get vital bridgeheads at lightning speed on the German side. Never had the element of surprise been so laboriously contrived and never had it been so valuable.

The Poles who had been forced to start their attack some hundreds of yards away from the floodbanks which were both held by the Germans were beset all round by minefields and did not make such good progress initially. Indeed it might be wondered that they had any heart for the battle at all because not only were they still recovering from the shock of the Yalta decision but the incident then occurred when during the preparatory bombardment some medium bombers dropped their loads far too short and they exploded right among the Poles forming up to the attack. Heavy casualties resulted.

It was then that General McCreery who had witnessed this dreadful incident through his binoculars from his command observation post with General Mark Clark recalled : 'I was horrified and I knew that General Anders would be very upset. Imagine my surprise when next time the chance of support from the medium bombers arose General Anders said, "Don't worry. I'll have them. They are not likely to make the same mistake twice." The gallant Poles were not dismayed and they soon made up for lost time.'

The attack which started at 7.20 pm was supported by one thousand five hundred guns of all types. For the first time flame throwing tanks were used and they annihilated many an enemy strong point. Gaps were blown in the floodbank to enable tanks to get up to the river and lower fascines – giant bundles of sticks – into it to form a bridge. This sufficed to get some armour over until more permanent bridges could be erected. But all the way a mass of obstacles was met and the white tapes laid by the sappers and infantry to guide us through the intricate minefields seemed endless.

For twenty-four hours the fiercest fighting took place but then two things happened which had an enormous influence on the outcome. Firstly, the Allies stepped up a gigantic concentration of support from the air on a segment of the Santerno River – the next obstacle. Pumping bullets and bombs into an area of about ten square miles no less than one thousand two hundred aircraft of all types laid a carpet of desolation in front of our troops which speeded their inexorable march. General Reinhardt, commanding the German 98th Division, veterans of the combat against the Russians in the Crimea, had never seen anything like it. He reported that lone despatch riders, even individual soldiers, were attacked from the air, and single tanks were bombarded by as many as a dozen aircraft at a time. Worse still from his point of view the Luftwaffe were shot out of the skies.

Secondly, Hitler had issued an order which had the profoundest effect on the battle. It was an order which defied the advice of his generals who, sensing the Allied breakthrough, wished to make an orderly retreat behind the various river obstacles until finally the shelter of the River Po was reached. The Führer decreed that every soldier should stand and fight.

This meant that as the New Zealanders, Poles, Gurkhas, Royal Fusiliers, Argylls and men of the Royal West Kents edged their way forward they started to isolate the enemy into small pockets, then bigger pockets and then into deep salients. The forward surge gathered momentum, the bridgeheads got larger, more and more tanks came over and then to add to the confusion a brigade of the 56th Division crossed the flooded ground in amphibious tanks on the enemy's left and landed there miles behind their lines at a place called Menate.

General von Schwerin commanding the Panzer corps divulged afterwards that he had thought this flooded area to be absolutely impassable and added bitterly that there had been a vital photograph showing about fifty amphibious tanks on the move – what a target for the Luftwaffe! – but it only reached him twenty-four hours after the attack had been made.

This waterborne assault took the British forward in a direct line for the Argenta Gap, the very hinge of the German defence strategy. Against fanatical resistance the brigades of 56th (London) Division, men of the London Irish, London Scottish, the Royal Fusiliers, Queens Royal Regiment (West Surrey), the Buffs, the Coldstream and Scots Guards all advanced yard by agonising yard.

Then the crack 78th British Division – Lancashire Fusiliers, East Surreys, Northamptons, the Buffs, Queen's Own Royal West Kents, Argylls and the Irish Brigade, burst through a bridgehead on the Santerno, wheeled right – due north – and with a lightning strike they captured a bridge across the Reno which the enemy had only partially destroyed. They were now also in line to go for that glittering prize – McCreery's obsession – the Argenta Gap.

In five days the Eighth Army had broken through all the major river defences that stood between them and the River Po. Thousands of prisoners had been taken. The enemy were fighting magnificently but they were still being out-fought and out-manoeuvred.

On 14th April, the day the 78th Division crossed the Reno, Vietinghoff, the German Commander-in-Chief, did two things which were really sensible. Realising at last that there was no danger of an attack by sea in his rear he moved his 29th Panzer Grenadiers Division forward over the Po to strengthen the defences of the vital Argenta Gap.

He then sent a heartfelt plea to Hitler to be allowed to fight a well-organised rearguard action and then withdraw his armies intact behind the River Po. The Führer took three days to send his reply and in those 72 hours events moved so fast that even if he had said 'yes' (which he didn't) it is doubtful if Vietinghoff could have achieved his purpose.

At a quarter to ten in the morning of 14th April General Truscott's Fifth Army attacked with enormous artillery and air support. Here again our four generals pulled off a coup because by allowing a five day time lag between the Eighth and Fifth Army efforts all the aircraft and much of the artillery could be concentrated on each front in turn and so get things off to what might aptly be called a 'flying start'.

For example, on the next day, 15th April, the air force put up a record by depositing one thousand five hundred tons of bombs on the enemy facing the Fifth Army advance, and another eight hundred tons on the rear areas.

The rousing rumbustious American GI's, the Brazilians, and the South Africans, battled through the mountains which stood between them and the Po valley. It was a slow bitter slog to begin with but every German soldier who stood and fought it out was less likely to be in a position to continue effective resistance later on.

By the 15th the Fifth Army was little more than ten miles from Bologna and Bologna was to the Fifth Army what Argenta was to the Eighth. In the next two days both armies launched the attacks which shattered the German defences.

The two British divisions, 78th and 56th, again with powerful air support, stormed through the Argenta Gap. So preoccupied were the Germans with the weight and speed of the attack that they only had time to organise themselves into battle groups. They had not even removed some of the 'Achtung Minen' notices which were posted around the perimeters of the minefields to warn their garrison in more leisurely days. It was not easy. In fact it was bloody, but in just two days the British soldiers fought their way through one of the most fiercely defended 'corridors' of all time. There were mines by the thousand to avoid, floods to wade through, enormous river banks to scale, pill boxes to subdue, and the rubble of the pounded houses to clamber over. There was mortar fire, enfilading machine gun fire, salvoes from self-propelled guns and bitter hand to hand street fighting to survive. It was a prodigious battle.

One of the key points was Argenta Railway Station where at the height of the conflict it is alleged one Tommy could be heard shouting suitable announcements. 'The next train will call at Oxshott, Bagshott, Bloodshot and all the other bloody stations down the line'.

According to General Mark Clark the breakthrough at Argenta was 'quite outstanding, achieved as it was against some of the best troops of the German army in formidable natural positions, strengthened throughout the winter months with all the ingenuity and thoroughness of the German High Command.'

Vietinghoff was now in a mess. Argenta – his vital hinge – had been sheared right off and already the door of his defences was swaying almost out of control under the thunderous knocks of the 5th Army. He wanted to withdraw but an answer to his plea to do so came back from Jodl on 17th April which put him right 'on the spot'. The telegram said :

All further proposals for a change in the present war strategy will be discontinued. I wish to point out particularly that under no circumstances must troops or commanders be allowed to waver or to adopt a defeatist attitude, as a result of such ideas apparently held in your headquarters. Where any such danger is likely, the sharpest counter-measures must be employed. The Führer expects, now as before, the utmost steadfastness in the fulfilment of your present mission, to defend every inch of the North Italian areas entrusted to your command. I desire to point out the serious consequences for all those higher commanders, unit commanders or staff officers who do not carry out the Führer's orders to the last word.

Despite the threat in the telegram Vietinghoff had the courage to order the general retreat to the Po on 20th April, but it was too late, far too late. The next day the GI's and the indefatigable Poles entered Bologna and with the Eighth Army pressing all along the line and debouching out of the Argenta Gap the scene was set for a fantastic finale.

Every unit, every nationality, every supporting element of the Fifth and Eighth Armies, careered towards the Po slashing the enemy with sweeping cuts as from a scimitar. The jabs and thrusts re-registered hourly on the battle maps resembled long tenuous fingers stretching right through the enemy lines. Our flanks were often exposed and it was not unusual for pockets of the enemy to appear in our rear echelon areas so quickly had our battle columns passed them. Often small parties of tired 'Teds' – special Eighth Army nickname for Germans derived from the Italian word for them, *Tedeschi* – would lie low by day and at dusk would give themselves up to the first Allied soldier they saw. One Cockney cook, dishing up some stew to his platoon, noticed two dishevelled Huns stepping out of the undergrowth nearby and coming straight at him with their mess tins at the ready! 'Blimey,' he said indignantly, 'will somebody tell those perishers to get in line.'

The Germans met an element in their headlong and desperate retreat they had not met before. Not only were they pursued and harassed by day by mobile columns and tremendous fighter-bomber support that knocked them off the roads but they were overrun by night as well. All through the dark hours both tanks and infantry moved forward in the artificial twilight created by the reflection of searchlights in the clouds. This technique of producing a little light on the subject had been in existence for some time to illumine the nocturnal distribution of supplies in static positions – but now the searchlights cleverly directed their beams to enable obstacles that might hinder tanks or infantry to be seen just that little bit more quickly. It was this innovation which prompted General McCreery to tell me later, 'If Montgomery had used tanks with searchlights at El Alamein he would have annihilated Rommel's army completely.'

This non-stop twenty-four hour a day war of movement was the last straw for the enemy. Thousands of prisoners were taken every day and night. They had to abandon their lorries, tanks and guns. Those that were not abandoned were shot up by the Air Force and burnt out. Whole divisions and corps collapsed complete with their senior officers and staffs. Those who managed to get to the Po had to swim across – like General Heidrich commanding the Parachute Corps. But by now the battle was over. The 10th Mountain Division of the Eighth Army covered fifty-five miles in only two days to be the first to reach the River Po. They reached it at ten o'clock on the night of 22nd April – only thirteen days after the offensive had started.

The German propaganda taunt that nothing would be like the crossing of the River Po for death and destruction was true – but only for them. For the Allies the crossing was only a bridging exercise, a formality, and in the next few days the remnants of the 23 German Divisions were chased and cornered with hardly a shot being fired. By the end of April an army of over half a million men had been destroyed and Vietinghoff formally offered his complete and uncondi-tional surrender. This was signed at Alexander's HQ in Caserta on 29th April 1945 – and it brought about the total capitulation of all the enemy forces in Italy and Southern Austria which, taking into account all the combat and line of communication and garrison troops, were estimated to amount to nearly a million men.

13. 'As gallant an army as ever marched'

'Now their reward has come I am very glad it has
come at a time when it can be singled out. It
stands out. It brings to a conclusion the work of
as gallant an army as ever marched . . .'

WINSTON CHURCHILL,
Wednesday, May 2nd, 1945, in the House of Commons

In the sea of momentous events which took place in that April of 1945,
each soldier was a lonely island of uncomprehending isolation. One was
conscious only of what life held for one for the next ten minutes or
for the hour. One was never aware that while one was crouching in a
shell hole or trying to snatch some food or sleep, at that very moment
the Fifth Army had captured Bologna or a whole German battle group
complete with generals and their staffs were already walking into
captivity.

The ability of the German soldiers to fight on to the very end
compelled the utmost respect and admiration. They were immensely
brave and skilful. Throughout the whole of the Italian campaign they
had brought to a fine art the deployment of small highly mobile
formations of mixed weapons which could bring down incredible
concentrations of fire power on our advancing echelons. They included
at various times their Mark IV or Tiger Tanks with low slung high
velocity guns which could match or beat anything we had; a number of
half-track self-propelled 88 millimetre guns which for accuracy and
mobility were outstanding; brilliantly trained machine-gun detachments
using Spandaus whose short high-speed bursts of fire resembled the
ripping of corrugated cardboard, and 'Bazookas' which were very
effective against any armoured vehicles, and above all small units of
infantry whose marksmanship, resourcefulness, and mastery of
camouflage and tactics made them most formidable.

So it was that when I attended an 'O Group' conference at my Brigade HQ on 23rd April to receive orders for the actual crossing of the River Po itself I did not realise that victory was at hand. I looked around at the faces of the Brigadier and his staff and the other commanding officers and all I read with sinking heart was that they too were viewing this next confrontation with the enemy with what I can only describe as a melancholy fatalism. No matter about our recent incredible successes and the exhilaration of our forward surge, we knew from bitter experience that they counted for nothing. We know that as we launched our attack across the Po the enemy with their customary legerdemain would conjure up from nowhere more tanks, more self-propelled guns, more Nebelwerfers, and more Spandau teams to bring about the slaughter which their propaganda leaflets had depicted so graphically. It was not just one more bloody river to cross, it was *the* river.

I remember making notes about the required roles for my heavy mortar and medium machine gun platoons and I was just in the process of marking some map reference on a piece of talc with a chinagraph pencil when an orderly walked in and handed a message to the Brigade Major. He in turn handed it to the Brigadier. Their faces gave no hint of its import but for some reason an electrifying silence fell upon us. Several seconds elapsed while the Brigadier read it carefully a second time. Then, quite deadpan, he announced :

'Gentlemen there has been a change of plan. It will no longer be our task to force a crossing of the Po. Forward elements of both the Fifth and the Eighth Armies are already across. Bridgeheads have been established and enemy resistance is virtually nil.'

This news burst upon us with all the explosive power of a nuclear anti climax. Having been conditioned mentally for months in advance to the inevitability of that most horrific of all our battles, that on the River Po, we sat quite stunned. Nobody said anything. Slowly one by one we took leave of the Brigadier and moved off to bring the news to our respective units. It was a very strange feeling. On the one hand one felt a tremendous relief that one was not going to be called upon to carry out what one thought would be this awesome final offensive, and on the other there lurked a niggling sense of frustration that one had been deprived of the ultimate test.

It was then that my curiosity was born about the extraordinary battle which had just taken place. I started to collect documents and anecdotes from those taking part which helped to give me a bigger perspective and which ultimately led me to talk to the generals about it long after the war. Every battle is made up of a mosaic of a thousand little battles. That for the River Po was no exception. Some of the incidents were as bizarre as the overall battle itself.

The men of the 132 Field Regiment Royal Artillery went into action a mile or so from a place called Consandolo and surprised themselves by capturing on and around their gun sites no less than five German officers and fifty three other ranks. All these were identified as part of the artillery of the 42nd Jaeger Division. There cannot be many occasions in the history of war when one artillery unit was directly involved in capturing another. Normally their counter-battery activity would be confined to exchanging long distance salvos.

Our tank units had their hour too. The 9th Lancers exploiting the breakout from Ferrara to the Po on 24th April came under increasing fire from armour piercing shells. A great tank battle ensued. Three German Mark IV tanks were observed moving fast along a road about nine hundred yards away. A few minutes later 'B' Squadron 9th Lancers reported that two of them had been stopped in their tracks and were well and truly ablaze. The third had escaped but was spouting smoke from the rear. This third one was later found holed and abandoned some distance down the road. Sergeant Edmunds had scored a right and a left with two shots right through the turrets and Corporal Nicholls had disposed of the third. At nine hundred yards in the fog of war this was magnificent shooting. On clearing up on the following morning the 9th Lancers were able to say that not since Alamein had they had such a victory. Almost the entire strength of the 26th Panzers had been destroyed. Ten Mark IV tanks were knocked out by direct fire. The crews of eleven became so frightened that they baled out and set fire to their own tanks, while the crews of two more just gave themselves up. In addition they captured six self-propelled guns, two heavy mortars, and 230 prisoners.

The Royal Engineers never had a more demanding operation. Events moved so quickly that plans were formulated, effected, and counter-manded almost simultaneously. The administration problems were vast. So called simple matters like marrying a bulldozer with its transporter or getting oil to some mechanical equipment became conundrums. Something of the dogged perseverance and humour of the gallant 'Sapper' is enshrined in a quote from the diary of 256 Field Company Royal Engineers for 22nd April.

The Officer Commanding was sent to the wrong location of 11 Brigade. This is the third time he has been wrongly directed by higher formations in the last seven days. First time he blew up on a mine. Second time he underwent Spandau fire. This time since he was near Brigade he suffered only inconvenience and dust.

A sergeant of a unit of the 10th (US) Mountain Division whom I met early in May on a souvenir hunting expedition told me he had picked up a jeep north of Bologna which carried him in that fantastic dash for the Po. In the back of it was a camouflage net which he imagined covered a large heap of rations and petrol. He was so absorbed with getting on with the war that it was not until twenty hours had elapsed before he took a look. Instead of rations and petrol he found to his dismay and delight what he described as 'a beautiful brown eyed leggy blonde'. It appeared that she had decided the best way of rejoining her family in Verona was to smuggle a lift on the first vehicle she could find.

'Jeez,' said the sergeant, 'she was so lovely I offered her marriage on the spot. My big problem was keeping her away from the other guys. She accepted. While I was thinking about the consummation she went and disappeared. I never saw her again. You can't trust dames. Mind you, my wife wouldn't have been too pleased if I had brought her back with me.'

In the confusion other strange things were happening. As the Japanese-Americans were liberating the city of Turin, British cavalry regiments were already seizing abandoned German horses and organising within sight and sound of shot and shell a brisk afternoon's point-to-point. April is of course the right time of the year for this particularly British sport, and the war had restricted these activities at home.

Strange prisoners came in too. There were numbers from most of the occupied countries who had 'volunteered' to fight for the Germans. Among these was a whole division of Russians, 'the White Cossacks', who guarded the lines of communication. By allying themselves with the Germans they hoped to overthrow Stalin and his henchmen, which had been their aim ever since 1919. The rounding up and deportation of these unhappy people back to Russia in due course as a result of Stalin's insistence is an infamous chapter in British history. They were tricked into their return by false assurances and promises, and were largely massacred by Stalin as soon as they stepped on to Russian soil.

However, as previously mentioned, the Poles on the enemy side were so assiduous in coming over to join their countrymen that the army of General Anders despite some 25,000 casualties was numerically stronger at the end of the war than it was at the beginning of the campaign. Surely this was the strangest and most effective recruiting system of all. The confusion produced some laughable situations as well. Angus Ross, for example, who later became a leading and respected figure in the advertising scene in London but then serving with the King's Hussars was moving his tank up to the Po. He was edging forward very cautiously and not without considerable apprehension because these were times when so fluid was the battle that one never knew where the next blast of armour piercing shot would come from.

Slowly and carefully he manoeuvred round the corner which gave him his first sight of the great river. He was hit not by enemy shell fire as he expected but by sheer amazement. He could not believe his eyes. There in front of him, happy to greet him and to tell him that he could put his tank away, were some members of his own 'B' Echelon and their trucks. They were just awaiting the completion of a bridge before continuing their advance. This was a somewhat unnerving and humiliating experience for Angus because the 'B' Echelon boys invariably carried out their administration role, providing petrol, oil, water, ammunition, and spare parts, from a safe distance well behind the operational troops up front.

But this was perhaps not quite such a ridiculous confrontation as one I had in those last hectic days. I was in the vicinity of the Po di Volano, an area of narrow roads crossing a maze of ditches and dykes. I awoke at dawn very bleary-eyed and walked forward from my jeep leaving my batman and driver behind. Having gone about a hundred yards in search of what I thought was one of my platoon areas, I suddenly realised that I was surrounded by the thick morning mist. Visibility was down to about ten yards and I was very much alone. I stood still in order to take stock and to work out how I was going to find my way back. Suddenly the unmistakeable metallic sound of tank tracks coming towards me could be heard. I stepped forward confidently to meet it because the previous night our own tanks had been all around us. I felt sure this one was just an early riser like myself probably looking for a place for a nice brew-up of that beloved army beverage – hot tea laced with sweet condensed milk. As I waited in the middle of the road the comforting sound of the tracks grew louder and louder. This was obviously a very big tank indeed. Probably one of our Shermans I reflected.

Suddenly the mist parted and the terrible shape of a 60-ton Tiger Tank burst upon me. A young German officer, his head above the turret, was speaking very quietly into his 'inter-com' line to his crew

below. The tank ground to a sudden halt. I found myself gazing dwon
the muzzle of the longest and most vicious looking gun I have ever
seen. It could knock out any armour we had with one single high
velocity shell. It was the very latest and most menacing of Teutonic
weaponry. I looked at the German officer and he looked at me. We
were both dumbfounded.

Our respective reactions thereafter were so incompatible with
preconceived ideas about British and German characteristics they are
worth giving in just a little detail. What does one do when one is
alone in the mists of nowhere and looking down the barrel of a Tiger
tank gun while being covered at the same time from the lofty eminence
of the impregnable turret by a lynx-eyed product of the 'master race'?
Frankly I was paralysed. Panic must then have prompted me to make
an instinctive reflex which doubtless was sown in my subconscious mind
through endless drills on some distant and long-forgotten parade
ground. I solemnly unbuttoned my holster and drew my pistol!

What does a smart young audacious German tank officer do when
out of the blue he meets a lone bleary-eyed British officer standing in
the middle of nowhere and who confirms his stupidity by drawing his
pistol with a speed which would have given John Wayne enough time
to get off a hundred shots even allowing for re-loading? Well this one
obviously thought that it was a senseless waste of ammunition to put
a shell right through the idiotic British officer. There were alternatives.
He could have used his pistol or a machine gun. He could even have
ordered his tank forward and simply run over him. But he did none
of these things.

He looked at me with almost a hint of amusement as I struggled
with my pistol. He then pointed down at his big gun with the index
finger of his right hand. He was obviously making it clear that a Smith
& Wesson .38 calibre pistol versus an 88 mm high velocity gun was
simply no contest. To emphasise the point he raised the same index
finger and wagged it at me from right to left several times in the same
way that a parent admonishes a naughty child. I stood there transfixed.
This was not the war I had heard so much about. I felt I should be
killing someone or someone should be killing me. But no, this was
ridiculous. It was the sort of situation dreamed up only in Charlie
Chaplin movies.

He then gave some instructions to his crew and the tank spun round
and clanked away. As the mist started to envelop it my last glimpse
of the German officer, with the distinct sense of humour, was as he
turned round to give me a half salute. It was perhaps more of a

peremptory wave expressing a mixture of sentiments ranging from 'Next time don't be such a bloody fool' to 'Goodbye and good luck' or even 'Let's meet again when the war is over'. Whatever it meant I found myself waving back. As I said before, the whole thing was ridiculous.

And so it was that the tapestry of victory had countless little personal threads like these woven into it. Each man gave of his best never knowing what effect if any it could possibly have on the outcome. But on this occasion the combination of so much individual effort brought about a truly astonishing triumph. The arithmetic is interesting. The total Allied casualties from 9th April to 2nd May 1945 were 16,747. In the first fourteen days alone of this period the Germans lost approximately 67,000 of whom 35,000 were made prisoners, the majority surrendering to the Americans. Bearing in mind that the Allies had to do all the attacking the discrepancy in their favour is a remarkable tribute to the planning and execution of all their operations. This was not only true of this final battle but also for the Italian campaign throughout the whole of its twenty long weary months. On the German side the casualties totalled 536,000 and on the Allied 312,000.

Perhaps the final verdict on the Po battle was that produced by thousands of soldiers in one last defiant act. It was never lost on the GI or the Tommy that the word 'Po' could be connected with the chamber pot found underneath the bed. Consequently there was a universal desire to pee into the Po at the first opportunity. To be able to say that one had done just that was something to brag about and even recount to the family back home. There was hardly a man who did not overtly take advantage of the river crossing to add his quota, preferably down wind, to the waters.

General Mark Clark when he made his debut was accompanied by his customary team of reporters and photographers. Half way across he was seen fumbling with his flies. It was obvious he could not resist the urge either. Cameras clicked and shorthand notes were taken to record the momentous occasion. However, nothing wholly specific emerged about the incident. The General obviously felt that it was somewhat undignified for the Commander of the Fifteenth Army Group to be seen waving his penis about and had organised a little censorship subsequently to prevent the news from spreading.

He told me when we met at Charleston years later in answer to my question: 'Yes, of course I did. If nothing else, I felt that after all we had been through and the fear of God which the Po had put into us, the best thing to do was simply to piss on it. Don't quote me on that.' The fact that I am doing so will not be taken by him, I hope, as a grave breach of confidence. I thought that in a racy and succinct way it so summarised this amazing battle, it simply could not be left out.

On 2nd May news that Winston Churchill was to make an important announcement flashed around the House of Commons a few minutes before he entered the chamber at 7.21 to tell of the first major surrender in the West of nearly 1,000,000 enemy in Italy. MP's hurried in. The public gallery was well filled, but the Prime Minister had to wait six minutes until he could interrupt a debate on land requisitioned for the war. Part of the ritual was that the Serjeant-at-Arms had to march to the table of the House and place upon it the Mace which rests underneath when the House is in Committee. At 7.29 pm precisely when the Mace was on the table Churchill rose to speak amid an expectant cheer. He spread a large typewritten sheet of foolscap on the dispatch box before him. He read the first few factual paragraphs in his statement. Then he folded up the typewritten document, put it away with his horn rimmed spectacles, and without any further notes described what happened. This is what he said.

'I promised that I would come to the House if anything of major importance occurred, and I would ask your leave, Mr Speaker, and the indulgence of the House, to make a short statement. There has been a certain amount of matter issued continuously from tape machines, and I thought perhaps the House would like to hear a short account which I have received from Field-Marshal Sir Harold Alexander.

'Field-Marshal Alexander, the Supreme Allied Commander in the Mediterranean theatre of operations, has just announced that the land, sea and air forces commanded by Colonel-General Heinrich von Vietinghoff-Scheel, German Commander-in-Chief, South-West Command, and Commander-in-Chief of the army group "C", have surrendered unconditionally. The instrument of surrender was signed on Sunday afternoon, April 29, at the Allied Forces Headquarters at Caserta, by two German plenipotentiaries and by Lieutenant-General W. D. Morgan, Chief of Staff at Allied Forces Headquarters. The terms of surrender provided for the cessation of hostilities at 12 o'clock noon, GMT, on Wednesday, 2nd May, that is to say 2 o'clock by our time.

'But as all these matters are accompanied by many elements of uncertainty, it was not until effective confirmation was obtained by the actual orders issued to the troops from the German High Command that Field-Marshal Alexander issued the statement which has now come over the wireless. The territory under General von Vietinghoff-Scheel, South-West Command, includes northern Italy to the Isonzo river in the north-east, and the Austrian province of Vorariberg, Tyrol, and Salzburg, and portions of Carinthia and Styria. It is therefore, geographically, a surrender which puts us into very close touch with the position of the United States armies of the north.

'The fighting troops of the enemy include the remnants of 22 German divisions and six Italian Fascist divisions, but with the combat and echelon troops upon the lines of communication and throughout this territory, which they have held for so long, the total numbers who have surrendered to the Allies are estimated to amount to nearly 1,000,000 men.

'Not only has a vast area of territory, vital in its character, fallen into the hands of the Supreme Commander, Sir Harold Alexander, but the actual surrender which has taken place so far, comprising the numbers it does, constitutes, I believe, a record for the whole of this war – and cannot fail but to be helpful to the further events for which we are looking.

'This army in Italy, American and British composed, commanded by our trusted General and having under him General Mark Clark, a most efficient and daring American soldier, has had a marvellous record since they first landed in the peninsula. . . .

'What has made it particularly difficult and depressing for this army is the tremendous inroads which have been made upon it in order to help forward other great operations. In June and July of last year what very nearly amounted to an army was taken from this Command in Italy, while only a very small corresponding reduction took place on the enemy's side. Now quite recently, a few months ago, feeling that it would probably be beyond the strength of this army, so weakened, to make a decisive attack, we moved another large addition of divisions to the western front, and some others went to Greece.

'This army was an army stripped of its strength and facing an enemy force which for all the purposes of war must have been considered far stronger because it had the duty of defending mountain ranges and, afterwards, plains flooded by autumn and winter rains, and which certainly in the number of divisions, exceeded those which were left to attack. Moreover those forces left to attack, as I pointed out in my message of congratulation to Field-Marshal Alexander, were of so many different nations that only some personality of commanding qualities could have held them all and woven them all together.

'If you look over the whole list of those men who have fought, you will find, taking as we may our own contribution first – it was the largest – the British and British Indian divisions of the highest quality. In addition to the British divisions we had the Poles – who have always fought with the greatest loyalty; the New Zealanders – who have marched all the way from the beginning right up to the very spearpoint of the advance; the South African Armoured Division – who were very forward in the fray; the great forces of the United States – second in numbers only to our own. Then there have been the Brazilian forces, which have made their steady advances; a negro division of United States troops, which has also distinguished itself; the Jewish Brigade, which we formed a year or so ago, and which has fought in the front line with courage; and finally the Japanese of American birth, who entered Turin. Finally, there were the free Italians – who have played their part in clearing their country from the German Fascist yoke. All these forces, weakened as they had been, were not discouraged. Divided as they were by racial differences, they were united and resolved upon their purpose.

'Now their reward has come. I am very glad it has come at a time when it can be singled out. It stands out. It brings to a conclusion the work of as gallant an army as ever marched – and brings to a pitch of fame the military reputation of a commander who has always, I may say, enjoyed the fullest confidence of the House of Commons.'

It was appropriate that Churchill should have the last word. It was he, and his undeviating support for the Allied cause in Italy, that brought to a triumphant conclusion the Italian campaign culminating as it did in what is arguably the strangest battle of World War II, the battle for the River Po.

Appendices

Appendix A

OPERATIONS INSTRUCTION
NUMBER 4

Headquarters 15th Army Group
APO No 777, US Army
Florence, Italy
24 March 1945

Phase I operations contained herein confirm verbal instructions issued by Commanding General, 15th Army Group, to Army commanders at conference 18 March 1945. Instructions previously issued that are not in accordance with these instructions are cancelled.

1. The offensive directed by this operations instruction should result in a major disaster to the enemy, and consequently have an important effect on the prompt termination of hostilities. If fully successful, it should be of so crushing and thorough a nature that it will be the last coordinated offensive against German forces which the 15th Army Group will make. The attention of all ranks within the 15th Army Group should be called to the unprecedented opportunities which are provided at this time for dealing a mortal blow to the enemy and accelerating the day of victory. It is of vital importance that each individual who contributes to the offensive shall devote fully his energy and abilities to driving the attack home to the enemy wherever he may be found, so that the maximum number of German troops will be destroyed or captured. To this end it is directed that all commanders use every effective means to acquaint thoroughly the troops under their command with the opportunities that lie before them at this time, and that leadership be active throughout the operations to exploit fully every phase of the situation as it develops.

2. a. 15th Army Group will launch an all-out attack 10 April 1945 to destroy maximum number enemy forces south of the PO, force crossings of the PO River and capture VERONA. (Note: 15th Army

Group D Day will be the day on which Eighth Army launches its attack to cross the SENIO River.)

    b. 15th Army Group's operation will be divided into phases as follows :

        1) Phase I – The breaching of the SANTERNO River by Eighth Army and the debouchment of Fifth Army into the PO Valley; to include the capture or isolation of the city of BOLOGNA.

        2) Phase II – The break-through by either or both Armies to encircle German forces south of the PO River.

        3) Phase III – The crossing of the PO River and the capture of VERONA.

3. Phase I.
    a. Eighth Army will :

        1) Breach the SENIO and SANTERNO Rivers.

        2) Attack immediately after a bridgehead is established over the SANTERNO :
            a) In the direction of BASTIA.
            b) In the direction of BUDRIO.

        3) If the situation is favourable, launch an amphibious operation, combined with a parachute drop, to assist the ground forces to break through the ARGENTA Gap. (Note : Depending upon the success of operations to secure the ARGENTA Gap, the Commanding General, 15th Army Group, in consultation with the General Officer Commanding, Eighth Army, will make the decision that an attack on FERRARA is to be the main effort of Eighth Army with a secondary attack on BUDRIO.)

    b. Fifth Army will :

        1) Launch the main effort of 15th Army Group and attack with the mission of debouching into the PO Valley with a secondary mission of capturing or isolating the city of BOLOGNA. Fifth Army will be prepared to launch the first phase of its main attack on 24 hours notice after D + 2.

        2) Launch a preliminary attack to capture MASSA (P 9101) on D − 5. Be prepared on capture of MASSA to exploit toward LA SPEZIA.

    c. Priority for air support will be given initially to Eighth Army. When Fifth Army's main attack is launched, priority for air will be given to that attack. Air plans for support of these operations will be issued by MATAF.

    d. Notification of postponement of Eighth Army's D Day attack, due to unfavourable weather, will be given by this headquarters 24 hours in advance of H Hour.

    e. Inter-Army boundary : No change.

4. Phase II.

    a. Eighth Army will :

      1) Prevent enemy forces escaping northwards by seizing and holding key road ——— which dominate the main ——— over the river RENO, and the PO crossing areas at FERRARA and BONDENO.

      2) Make earliest possible contact with exploiting columns of Fifth Army in the BONDENO–FERRARA area.

      3) Send strong mobile columns of armor and infantry for this purpose directed on FERRARA and BONDENO with intermediate objectives PORTOMAGGIORE (M 2669) and S. NICOLO FERRARESE (M 1871), by way of the ARGENTA Gap.

    b. Fifth Army will :

      1) Exploit with armor and infantry in the corridor between the RENO and PANARO Rivers, with a view of joining Eighth Army at the earliest possible time in the BONDENO or FERRARA area, thereby completing the encirclement of enemy forces south of the PO River.

      2) Seize S. GIOVANNI (L 7765). Thence direct the main effort on CENTO (L 8574) – S. AGOSTINO (L 9381) – BONDENO, denying to the enemy crossings of the RENO River.

      3) Launch a secondary effort northwest from the S. GIOVANNI area to seize crossings of the PANARO River near BOMPORTO and CAMPOSANTO, thence to turn northward in the corridor between the PANARO and SECCHIA River, moving on OSTIGLIA.

    c. Inter-Army boundary: Present boundary thence CASTE-NASO (L 9949) – CASTEL MAGGIORE (L 9057) – ARGELATO (L 8964) – CASTELLO D'ARGILE (L 8669) – CENTO (L 8574) all inclusive to Eighth Army, thence exclusive to Eighth Army FINALE (L 8685) – CENSELLI (F 9205).

5. Phase III.

a. It is vitally important that both Armies be prepared to seize any opportunity to capture existing bridging and ferrying equipment useful in a crossing of the PO River. It is probable that such opportunities may occur during Phase II operations. In the event that any means of crossing are secured by forces of either Army, every effort will be made to establish a bridgehead over the river and to initiate the movement through this bridgehead of all available forces for the exploitation on VERONA.

b. If, upon reaching the PO River, suitable means of crossing are not available, reconnaissance of crossing sites will be begun and bridging equipment moved up as rapidly as possible.

c. In the event that bridging equipment must be brought forward and crossings over the PO River made against enemy opposition, additional instructions will be issued covering these operations.

d. Operations Instruction Number 3, this headquarters, dated 12 February 1945, states that as our attack progresses toward VERONA, and when enemy resistance in northwest Italy has lessened to a degree permitting, IV US Corps will be detached from Fifth Army for independent operations in northwest Italy. The instructions in Operations Instruction Number 3 remain current but are in no way intended to interfere with the employment of IV Corps in the main battle.

e. Separate instructions covering the occupation of northeast Italy will be issued shortly.

f. Inter-Army boundary : Later.

6. Naval Support.

a. The following measures are being taken by Royal Navy to assist 15th Army Group's offensive :

    1)   On East coast.

        a)   Prior to D Day, naval activity designed to simulate the preparation of an amphibious operation in the area of PORTO GARIBALDI.

        b)   At a date to be selected by Eighth Army after D Day, a demonstration by landing craft and light supporting units off PORTO GARIBALDI to support the cover plan. A small Commando raid will also be landed North of PORTO GARIBALDI if practicable.

    2)   On West coast.

Naval bombardment in support of Fifth Army's attack

along West coast. A demonstration by light naval craft off CHIAVARI to simulate a landing at a time to be selected by 15th Army Group.

b. Plans for Royal Navy operations will be issued separately.

7. Present enemy strengths and probable reaction to this operation issue separately.

By Command of Lieutenant General CLARK :

A. M. GRUENTHER
Major General, GSC
Chief of Staff

Official:

DONALD W. BRANN
Brigadier General, GSC
AC of S, G–3

Appendix B

ORDER OF BATTLE OF FIFTEENTH ARMY GROUP

As at 9th April, 1945

FIFTH (UNITED STATES) ARMY

Under Army Command
    85 (US) Infantry Division [Army reserve, Porretta area]
        337 Regimental Combat Team
        338 Regimental Combat Team
        339 Regimental Combat Team
    92 (US) Infantry Division [West coast sector]
        370 Regimental Combat Team
        442 (Japanese-American) Regimental Combat Team (attached)
        473 Regimental Combat Team (formerly Anti-Aircraft Artillery)
        (attached)

II (US) Corps [Monte Grande to Route 64]
    Legnano Combat Group
        68 (Italian) Infantry Regiment
        69 (Italian) Infantry Regiment
    34 (US) Infantry Division
        133 Regimental Combat Team
        135 Regimental Combat Team
        168 Regimental Combat Team
    88 (US) Infantry Division
        349 Regimental Combat Team
        350 Regimental Combat Team
        351 Regimental Combat Team
    91 (US) Infantry Division
        361 Regimental Combat Team
        362 Regimental Combat Team
        363 Regimental Combat Team

6 South African Armoured Division
  11 South African Armoured Brigade
    Prince Alfred's Guard
    Pretoria Regiment (Princess Alice's Own)
    Special Service Battalion
  12 South African Motor Brigade
    Royal Natal Carbineers
    First City/Capetown Highlanders
    Witwatersrand Rifles/Regiment de la Rey
  13 South African Motor Brigade
    Natal Mounted Rifles
    Royal Durban Light Infantry
    Imperial Light Horse/Kimberley Regiment

IV (US) Corps [Route 64 to east of Bagni di Lucca]
  1 (US) Armoured Division
    6 Armoured Infantry Battalion
    11 Armoured Infantry Battalion
    14 Armoured Infantry Battalion
    1 Tank Battalion
    4 Tank Battalion
    13 Tank Battalion
  10 (US) Mountain Division
    85 Mountain Infantry Regiment
    86 Mountain Infantry Regiment
    87 Mountain Infantry Regiment
  1 Brazilian Infantry Division
    1 (Brazilian) Infantry Regiment
    6 (Brazilian) Infantry Regiment
    11 (Brazilian) Infantry Regiment
  365 Regimental Combat Team
  371 Regimental Combat Team
    [Detached from 92 (US) Infantry Division]

EIGHTH (BRITISH) ARMY
5 (Br.) Corps [Adriatic to south of Lugo]
  56 (Br.) Infantry Division
    167 Infantry Brigade
      9 Battalion Royal Fusiliers
      1 Battalion London Scottish
      1 Battalion London Irish Rifles

24 Guards Brigade
  2 Battalion Coldstream Guards
  1 Battalion Scots Guards
  1 Battalion The Buffs (Royal East Kent Regiment)
169 Infantry Brigade
  2/5 Battalion Queens Royal Regiment (West Surrey)
  2/6 Battalion Queens Royal Regiment (West Surrey)
  2/7 Battalion Queens Royal Regiment (West Surrey)
Cremona Combat Group
  21 (Italian) Infantry Regiment
  22 (Italian) Infantry Regiment
8 Indian Infantry Division
  17 Indian Infantry Brigade
    1 Battalion Royal Fusiliers
    1 Battalion Frontier Force Regiment
    1 Battalion 5 Royal Gurkha Rifles (Frontier Force)
  19 Indian Infantry Brigade
    1 Battalion Argyll and Sutherland Highlanders
    3 Battalion 8 Punjab Regiment
    One Battalion of Jaipur State Infantry
    6 Battalion Royal Frontier Force Rifles
  21 Indian Infantry Brigade
    5 Battalion Queens Own Royal West Kent Regiment
    1 Battalion Mahratta Light Infantry
    3 Battalion 15 Punjab Regiment
78 (Br) Infantry Division
  11 Infantry Brigade
    2 Battalion Lancashire Fusiliers
    1 Battalion East Surrey Regiment
    5 Battalion Northamptonshire Regiment
  36 Infantry Brigade
    5 Battalion The Buffs (Royal East Kent Regiment)
    6 Battalion Queens Own Royal West Kent Regiment
    8 Battalion Argyll and Sutherland Highlanders
  38 (Irish) Infantry Brigade
    2 Battalion Royal Inniskilling Fusiliers
    1 Battalion Royal Irish Fusiliers
    2 Battalion London Irish Rifles
2 New Zealand Division
  4 New Zealand Armoured Brigade
    18 Battalion New Zealand Armoured Regiment

19 Battalion New Zealand Armoured Regiment
20 Battalion New Zealand Armoured Regiment
5 New Zealand Infantry Brigade
   21 Battalion New Zealand Regiment
   23 Battalion New Zealand Regiment
   28 Battalion (Maori) New Zealand Regiment
6 New Zealand Infantry Brigade
   24 Battalion New Zealand Regiment
   25 Battalion New Zealand Regiment
   26 Battalion New Zealand Regiment
9 New Zealand Infantry Brigade
   2 Battalion New Zealand (Cavalry) Regiment
   22 Battalion New Zealand Regiment
   27 Battalion New Zealand (Machine Gun) Regiment
2 Armoured Brigade
  Queens Bays
  9 Queens Royal Lancers
9 Armoured Brigade
  27 Lancers (less one squadron)
  755 (US) Tank Battalion
   LVsT (Fantails)
21 Tank Brigade
  12 Battalion Royal Tank Corps
  48 Battalion Royal Tank Corps
  1 North Irish Horse
2 Commando Brigade
  2 Commando
  9 Commando
  40 Royal Marine Commando
  45 Royal Marine Commando

2 Polish Corps [Astride Route 9]
  3 Carpathian Division
   1 Carpathian Brigade
    1 Carpathian Rifle Battalion
    2 Carpathian Rifle Battalion
    3 Carpathian Rifle Battalion
   2 Carpathian Rifle Brigade
    4 Carpathian Rifle Battalion
    5 Carpathian Rifle Battalion
    6 Carpathian Rifle Battalion

   3 Carpathian Rifle Brigade
     7 Carpathian Rifle Battalion
     8 Carpathian Rifle Battalion
     9 Carpathian Rifle Battalion
 5 Kresowa Division
   4 Wolynska Infantry Brigade
     10 Wolynska Rifle Battalion
     11 Wolynska Rifle Battalion
     12 Wolynska Rifle Battalion
   5 Wilenska Infantry Brigade
     13 Wilenska Rifle Battalion
     14 Wilenska Rifle Battalion
     15 Wilenska Rifle Battalion
   6 Lwowska Infantry Brigade
     16 Lwowska Rifle Battalion
     17 Lwowska Rifle Battalion
     18 Lwowska Rifle Battalion
 2 Polish Armoured Brigade
   1 Battalion Polish Amoured Cavalry Regiment
   4 Battalion Polish Armoured Regiment
   6 Battalion Lwowska Armoured Regiment
 7 Armoured Brigade
   6 Battalion Royal Tank Corps
   8 Battalion Royal Tank Corps
 43 Indian Lorried Infantry Brigade
   2 Battalion 6 Gurkha Rifles
   2 Battalion 8 Gurkha Rifles
   2 Battalion 10 Gurkha Rifles
   14/20 Hussars
   2 Battalion Royal Tank Corps

10 (Br) Corps [Exclusive Route 9 to south of Imola]
 Jewish Infantry Brigade Group
   1 Battalion Palestine Regiment
   2 Battalion Palestine Regiment
   3 Battalion Palestine Regiment
 Friuli Combat Group
   87 Italian Infantry Regiment
   88 Italian Infantry Regiment

13 (Br) Corps [South of Imola to Monte Grande]
Folgore Combat Group
Nembo Regiment
S. Marco Regiment
(Bafile, Grado and Caorle Battalions)
10 Indian Infantry Division
10 Indian Infantry Brigade
1 Battalion Durham Light Infantry
2 Battalion 4 Gurkha Rifles
4 Battalion Baluch Regiment
One Battalion of the Jodhpur Sardar Infantry
20 Indian Infantry Brigade
2 Battalion Loyal Regiment
3 Battalion Mahratta Light Infantry
2 Battalion 3 Gurkha Rifles
1 Battalion 2 Punjab Regiment
One Battalion of Nabha Akal Infantry
Lovat Scouts
2 Battalion Highland Light Infantry
25 Indian Infantry Brigade
1 Battalion Kings Own Royal Regiment
3 Battalion 1 Punjab Regiment
3 Battalion Royal Garhwal Rifles
4 Battalion 11 Sikhs

ARMY RESERVE
6 (Br) Armoured Division
26 Armoured Brigade
16/5 Lancers
17/21 Lancers
2 Lothians and Border Horse
1 Guards Brigade
3 Battalion Grenadier Guards
3 Battalion Welsh Guards
1 Battalion The Welch Regiment
61 Infantry Brigade
1 Battalion Kings Royal Rifle Corps
2 Battalion Rifle Brigade
7 Battalion Rifle Brigade

2 Parachute Brigade
    4 Parachute Battalion
    5 Parachute Battalion
    6 Parachute Battalion

Appendix C

ORDER OF BATTLE OF ARMY GROUP 'C'

As at 9th April, 1945

ARMY GROUP RESERVE
90 Panzer Grenadier Division [SW of Modena]

TENTH ARMY
LXXVI Panzer Corps [Adriatic coast to north of Route 9]
 162 (Turkoman) Infantry Division
 42 Jaeger Division
 362 Infantry Division
 98 Infantry Division
I Parachute Corps [Route 9 to Monte Grande]
 26 Panzer Division
 4 Parachute Division
 278 Infantry Division
 1 Parachute Division
 305 Infantry Division
LXXIII Corps [Venice area]
 Minor defensive units only
XCVII Corps (i) [North-eastern Italy]
 188 Mountain Division
 237 Infantry Division
Army Reserve [Area Venice-Treviso]
 29 Panzer Grenadier Division
 155 Infantry Division

FOURTEENTH ARMY
XIV Panzer Corps [Monte Grande to Route 64]
 65 Infantry Division

8 Mountain Division (ii)
94 Infantry Division
LI Mountain Corps [Route 64 to Tyrrhenian coast]
   334 Infantry Division
   114 Jaeger Division
   232 Infantry Division
   Italia Infantry Division
   148 Infantry Division
 (i) Transferred to Army Group 'E' on 10th April, 1945.
(ii) 157 Mountain Division renumbered.

ARMY LIGURIA
Corps Lombardy [Coast of the Gulf of Genoa]
   San Marco Infantry Division
   Battle Group Meinhold [Genoa]
LXXV Corps [Franco-Italian frontier]
   34 Infantry Division
   Littorio Infantry Division
   5 Mountain Division
   Monte Rosa Mountain Division

Total Divisions in Army Group 'C'

GERMAN			ITALIAN		
Armoured Division	...	1	Infantry Divisions	...	3
Motorised Divisions	...	2	Mountain Division	...	1
Parachute Divisions	...	2			
Mountain, Jaeger and					
Infantry Divisions	...	18			
Total ...	...	23	Total ...	...	4

Appendix D

SOME OF THE BRITISH UNITS OF THE 8th ARMY
IN THEIR FINAL BATTLE – APRIL 1945

1st and 9th Royal Fusiliers
1st London Scottish
1st and 2nd London Irish Rifles
2nd Coldstream Guards
1st Scots Guards
1st and 5th The Buffs
1st Princess Louise's Kensington Regiment
2/5, 2/6, 2/7 Queens Royal Regiment (West Surrey)
6th Cheshire
1st and 8th Argyll & Sutherland Highlanders
5th and 6th Queens Own Royal West Kent
2nd Lancashire Fusiliers
1st East Surrey
5th Northampton
1st Royal Irish Fusiliers
2nd Royal Inniskilling Fusiliers
1st Durham Light Infantry
2nd Highland Light Infantry
1st Kings Own Royal Regiment
3rd Grenadier Guards
3rd Welsh Guards
1st The Welsh Regiment
21st Tank Brigade
Queens Bays
9th Queens Royal Lancers
2nd Lothian & Border Horse
44th and 56th Reconnaissance Regiment

1st KRRC

2nd and 7th Rifle Brigade

4th, 5th, 6th Parachute Battalions

2nd and 9th Commando and 40th and 45th Royal Marine Commando

Units of the Middlesex Regiment, North Irish Horse, Royal Tank
Corps, Hussars, Lancers

Among the Royal Artillery Units were : 17, 64, 65, 113, 132, 138, 152,
154 Field Regiments

64, 67 and 72 Anti Tank Regiments and 12 RHA

Among the Royal Engineers were : 214, 220, 221, 237, 256 and 501
Field Companies

281 and 563 Field Park Companies

8 and 625 Field Squadrons

144 Field Park Squadron

Appendix E

FROM : HQ 15 ARMY GROUP
TO :   (1)   FIFTH ARMY
          (2)   EIGHTH ARMY
INFO :   (3)   AFHQ*
          (4)   MATAF (by hand)†
Orig. No. o—5430

DATE/TOO 231600 B

TOPSEC (.) 15TH ARMY GROUP CONTINUES THE ATTACK TO DESTROY THE ENEMY (.) EIGHTH ARMY AFTER CROSSING THE RIVER PO WILL PUSH RAPIDLY FORWARD TO BREACH THE ADIGE POSITION AND CAPTURE PADUA (.) FIFTH ARMY WILL CONTINUE THE ATTACK WITH ITS MAIN EFFORT ON VERONA (.) A SECONDARY EFFORT WILL BE DIRECTED ON THE AXIS BERGAMO K. 6387—COMO E. 1902 TO DENY THE ENEMY ESCAPE ROUTES TO THE NORTH (.) AFTER REACHING VERONA TO BE PREPARED TO TURN EAST TO CROSS THE RIVER ADIGE NORTH OF LEGNANO AND ASSIST THE ADVANCE OF EIGHTH ARMY (.) BOUNDARY (.) ALL POINTS INCLUSIVE TO FIFTH ARMY (.) CENESELLI F. 9206—F. 932091—THENCE ALONG CAVO BENTIVOGLIO TO F. 870133—RIVER AT F. 870148—BR F. 851223— THENCE ALONG SCOLO LAVIGNO TO F. 840283—RIVER ADIGE AT F. 865295 (.) ACKNOWLEDGE.

---

* Allied Forces HQ (ie Field Marshal Alexander's HQ).
† Allied Air Force Tactical Command.

Appendix F

FROM : HQ 15 ARMY GROUP   DATE/TOO 261355 B
TO :   (1)   FIFTH ARMY Personal to TRUSCOTT
                from CLARK
    (2)   EIGHTH ARMY Personal to McCreery
                from CLARK
INFO : (3)   AFHQ   (6)   FONALI
      (4)   CG MATAF (by hand) (7)   No. 1 DISTRICT
      (5)   CG PBS   (8)   No. 2 DISTRICT
ORIG. NO. 0—5450

TOPSEC (.)   SUBJECT FUTURE OPERATIONS (.)
PARA ONE (.)   15 ARMY GROUP MISSION REMAINS TO DESTROY ENEMY IN ITALY (.)
PARA TWO (.)   EIGHTH ARMY WILL PAREN* ABLE PAREN PUSH RAPIDLY FORWARD BREACH ADIGE DEFENSE LINE AND CAPTURE PADUA (.) PAREN* BAKER PAREN BE PREPARED TO ADVANCE ON AXIS TREVISO—UDINE—TRIESTE (.)
PARA THREE (.)   FIFTH ARMY WILL PAREN ABLE PAREN AS PRIMARY EFFORT CROSS ADIGE RIVER FROM INGL LEGNANO NORTHWARD AND ADVANCE RAPIDLY ON VICENZA (.) ON SEIZING VICENZA BE PREPARED ON ARMY GROUP ORDER TO ADVANCE ON PADUA AND/OR TREVISO TO ENCIRCLE ENEMY FACING EIGHTH ARMY PAREN BAKER PAREN AS SECONDARY EFFORT DISPATCH

* Abbreviation for parenthesis (a) and (b).

FORCES ON AXIS BERGAMO—COMO TO DENY ENEMY ESCAPE ROUTES TO NORTH (SEE OUR MESSAGE 0—5430 APRIL 23) THESE FORCES MAY ENCOUNTER INTEGRATED ENEMY FORMATIONS WITHDRAWING FROM ITALO-FRANCO FRONTIER (.) EVERY EFFORT WILL BE MADE TO REACH COMO EARLIEST AND PREVENT ENEMY ESCAPE TO GERMANY (.) PAREN CHARLIE PAREN AT SUCH TIME AS IT WILL NOT INTERFERE WITH MISSIONS GIVEN IN

Index

Index